The Easy to Follow
SLOW COOKER COOKBOOK

Creative and Effortless Recipes to Help You Stay on Top of
Your Busy Schedule Without Breaking the Bank!

Bethany Berry

Index

Introduction

Welcome dear readers to my new book, The Easy to Follow Slow Cooker Cookbook!

I'm so delighted to have you join me on this journey into the wonderful world of slow cooking. My name is Bethany and I've been a professional chef for over 15 years. But my real passion is creating magical, fuss-free meals using an old faithful friend: the slow cooker. This handy appliance has been part of my kitchen for as long as I can remember. I first started using a slow cooker years ago when my grandmother gifted me her vintage 1970s avocado green crockpot. I was a broke culinary school student at the time and became immediately obsessed with the convenience. I'd prep a meal in the morning and come home to a ready-made dinner of melt-in-your-mouth pot roast or the most luscious spaghetti sauce. Over the years I've truly mastered the technique of slow cooking and learned how remarkably versatile it can be.

From rich stews to decadent cheesecakes, this appliance can do it all with such simple, hands-off ease. In this book I'm thrilled to share all my secrets and signature recipes I've developed as an executive chef and through decades of at-home slow cooking for my family. You'll find an array of delicious recipes from snacks and appetizers to main courses and even cocktails and desserts. I'll teach you tips to save time, shop smart, and adapt traditional recipes. With my guidance, you'll gain confidence using your slow cooker and be able to create amazing meals with minimal fuss. So welcome aboard! I can't wait for you to discover the art of set-it-and-forget-it cooking. Let's begin our slow cooking adventure!

We used some icons to make your reading experience more fun:

 Preparation Time

 Cooking Time

 Servings

What you will find in this book

In the pages of this book, I will guide you through effectively using your slow cooker to whip up a wide range of crave-worthy meals with true ease. We'll start with the basics, reviewing how to properly care for and use your slow cooker to get the most out of this appliance. I'll explain each temperature setting in detail so you can confidently achieve the optimal cooking time for different dishes. You'll learn pro tips and tricks for prepping ingredients specifically for the slow cooker so flavors develop beautifully. I'll share my proven techniques for layering components to cook thoroughly without drying out. You'll discover how to adapt traditional recipes into delicious slow cooker meals with my easy formula. I'll offer helpful guidelines on cook times for various meats and vegetables so your dishes come out perfect every time. You'll find a treasury of my family's cherished slow cooker recipes that I crafted over the years ranging from comforting soups and stews to flavorful chicken, pork and beef main dishes, to surprising appetizers and divine desserts you can make start to finish in the slow cooker. I'll troubleshoot any problems you may encounter and give tips to avoid common slow cooking mistakes. With this book as your guide, you'll gain the confidence, skills, and inspiration to fully harness the magic of the slow cooker to simplify cooking and enjoy mouthwatering "set it and forget it" meals for any occasion!

What is a slow cooker?

For those unfamiliar, a slow cooker is a countertop electric appliance used to simmer food at low temperatures for prolonged periods of time. At the heart of a slow cooker is a removable stoneware insert, usually encased in an electric heating base. This insert is where the magic happens. The stoneware retains and evenly distributes heat, ensuring that every morsel of your meal is cooked to perfection. The lidded design of the slow cooker plays a crucial role as well, as it traps heat and moisture, creating a self-contained cooking environment that infuses your dishes with rich flavors and keeps them moist and tender. Slow cookers cook food gently using minimal electricity over the course of several hours. The automatic settings switch to warm after the cook time is complete so food stays hot and ready to eat. This hands-off approach allows you to prep ingredients in the morning or the night before and then come home to a complete, piping hot meal with no additional work.

The benefits are endless:

- **Hands-off Convenience**: The hallmark of a slow cooker is its ability to do the cooking for you. Once you've prepared your ingredients and set the temperature and timer, you can walk away and attend to other tasks while your meal slowly simmers to perfection.
- **Cooks While You're Away**: Whether you're at work, running errands, or simply relaxing, your slow cooker continues to work diligently, ensuring that dinner is ready when you are.
- **Timed Settings**: Many slow cookers come equipped with programmable timers and automatic temperature settings, allowing you to precisely control the cooking process. This ensures that your food is neither undercooked nor overdone.
- **Energy Efficient**: Slow cookers are remarkably energy-efficient compared to traditional oven or stovetop cooking methods. They use a fraction of the electricity while producing equally scrumptious results.

- **Tenderizes Inexpensive Cuts of Meat**: One of the slow cooker's secret talents is its ability to transform tough, inexpensive cuts of meat into tender, succulent dishes. It achieves this by breaking down collagen over extended cooking times.
- **Keeps Food Piping Hot and Ready to Eat**: After cooking, slow cookers automatically switch to a "keep warm" setting, ensuring that your meal stays hot and ready to serve whenever you're ready to dig in.
- **Simple Cleanup**: Cleaning up after a slow-cooked meal is a breeze. Most slow cooker inserts are removable and dishwasher-safe, making cleanup almost as effortless as cooking.

How to take care of your slow cooker

Caring properly for your slow cooker will help it last for years while performing optimally. Be sure to read the manufacturer's instructions for specific guidelines, but here are my top tips: Wash the removable insert, lid, and heating base after each use by hand or in the dishwasher. Avoid abrasive scouring pads on the stoneware; a soft sponge or brush cleans effectively. Completely dry all parts and don't return the insert or lid to the base when wet. This can damage the heating element over time. Check for cracks; small fissures in the insert can expand during heating. Replace any damaged pieces. Between uses, store the lid off the insert and leave the base unplugged. This prevents accidentally turning it on and improves airflow to discourage bacteria growth. Periodically wipe the base heating unit with a dry cloth to keep it free of dust and debris which can obstruct ventilation. Descale hard water stains by filling the insert with equal parts vinegar and water and running a heat cycle. Use oven mitts when handling the hot insert. Avoid sudden temperature changes which can crack the stoneware; don't add cold water to a very hot insert. Don't use abrasive scouring pads or metal utensils that can scratch the insert surface. Clean up dried-on food right after cooking; it gets harder to remove once dried. With regular cleaning and proper care, your slow cooker should serve you reliably for many years!

Tips and tricks

Getting the most out of your slow cooker is a culinary journey filled with convenience and delicious rewards, but it also requires some finesse to avoid common pitfalls. Here, I'll share an extensive array of tips to help you harness the full potential of your slow cooker while sidestepping those all-too-familiar mistakes.

- **Spray the Insert**: Start with a simple but effective tip: lightly spray the inside of your slow cooker's stoneware insert with cooking oil or use slow cooker liners. This will not only prevent sticking but also make cleanup a breeze.
- **Layer Ingredients Properly**: For even cooking, it's crucial to layer your ingredients properly. Place root vegetables and denser items at the bottom and meats on top. This arrangement ensures that everything cooks evenly, leaving no undercooked or overcooked bits.
- **Keep the Lid On**: The lid plays a pivotal role in retaining moisture and maintaining a consistent cooking temperature. Resist the urge to lift the lid frequently; doing so can significantly extend cooking times. Trust that the slow cooker is doing its job.
- **Avoid Overfilling**: Overfilling your slow cooker can lead to uneven cooking and messy spills. To ensure proper circulation of heat and a well-cooked meal, fill the slow cooker no more than two-thirds full.

- **Use Correct Cooking Times**: Each recipe in your slow cooker cookbook will have recommended cooking times and settings. Pay close attention to these guidelines, as different dishes require varying cook times and temperature settings.
- **Adapt Traditional Recipes**: Slow cookers are incredibly versatile, but adapting traditional recipes may be necessary. Reduce the liquid content as slow cookers don't experience the same evaporation rate as stovetop cooking. Thickening agents like flour or cornstarch can be added towards the end of the cooking process to achieve the desired consistency.
- **Avoid Cramming Too Much Food**: While it's tempting to maximize your slow cooker's capacity, cramming too much food inside can lead to subpar results. Overcrowding impedes the circulation of heat, resulting in uneven cooking. If you need to cook large quantities, consider using multiple slow cookers or cooking in batches.
- **Get the Right Liquid Ratio**: Achieving the perfect liquid balance is crucial. There should be enough liquid to cover the ingredients, ensuring they remain moist and tender. However, too much liquid can lead to a soupy outcome. It's often best to start with less and add more if needed during the cooking process.
- **Food Safety Tips**: Always prioritize food safety. Start with proper thawing of frozen ingredients before adding them to your slow cooker. For meats, ensure they reach a safe internal temperature to kill any harmful bacteria. Follow recommended cooking times closely to achieve both safety and flavor.
- **Prep in Advance**: To streamline your slow cooking experience, prep ingredients in advance. Chop vegetables, trim meats, and measure out seasonings ahead of time. This not only saves you time on busy days but also ensures a smoother cooking process.

With these tips in your culinary arsenal, you'll maximize the potential of your slow cooker and navigate the path to flavorful, hassle-free meals. The key is patience and practice, and soon, you'll be orchestrating culinary masterpieces with ease, making your slow cooker an indispensable tool in your kitchen.

Overnight Steel Cut Oats

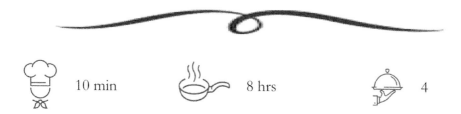

10 min   8 hrs   4

Ingredients:

- 200g steel cut oats
- 950ml water
- 240ml milk
- 30ml honey
- 5ml vanilla extract
- 1g salt
- 300g mixed berries (fresh or frozen)

Directions:

1. Oil your slow cooker using cooking spray.
2. In your slow cooker, combine steel cut oats, water, milk, honey, vanilla extract, and salt. Set it to low temp, then cook within eight hours overnight.
3. In the morning, gently stir the cooked oats and add in mixed berries. Let it warm within few minutes.
4. Serve hot, divided among four bowls. Feel free to garnish with extra berries or a drizzle of honey if desired.

Nutritional Values:

- Calories: 342
- Net Carbs: 59g
- Fat: 7g
- Protein: 12g
- Sugar: 5g

Difficulty: 1 2 3 4 5

Bacon and Spinach Frittata

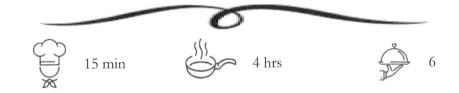

15 min   4 hrs   6

Ingredients:

- 200g bacon, chopped
- 200g spinach, chopped
- Twelve big eggs
- 100ml whole milk
- Salt & pepper, as required
- 5ml olive oil
- 100g cheddar cheese, grated
- 200g cherry tomatoes, halved

Directions:

1. Cook the bacon on moderate temp in your pan till crispy. Remove, then put aside.
2. In your big container, whisk eggs and milk. Flavour it using salt plus pepper. Mix in cooked bacon, chopped spinach, cheese, and cherry tomatoes.
3. Grease your slow cooker with olive oil, then add egg mixture.
4. Cook on low within four hours till centre is set. Carefully remove the frittata, then gently lifting it out.
5. Slice into six servings.

Nutritional Values:

- Calories: 345
- Net Carbs: 5g
- Fat: 21g
- Protein: 32g
- Sugar: 2g

Difficulty: **1** 2 3 4 5

French Toast Casserole

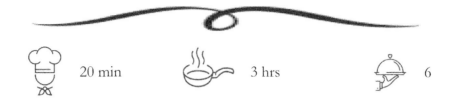

🧑‍🍳 20 min   🍳 3 hrs   🍽 6

Ingredients:

- 400g French bread, sliced & cubed
- Six big eggs
- 300ml whole milk
- 100ml double cream
- 50g granulated sugar
- 10ml pure vanilla extract
- 3g ground cinnamon
- Salt, as required
- 100g light brown sugar, for topping
- 50g unsalted butter, melted, for topping

Directions:

1. Oil your slow cooker using non-stick cooking spray. Arrange the cubed French bread evenly on your slow cooker.
2. In your big container, whisk eggs, milk, double cream, granulated sugar, vanilla extract, cinnamon, plus salt. Pour egg mixture over the bread cubes.
3. In your small container, mix light brown sugar plus melted butter.
4. Drizzle brown sugar-butter mixture on your bread. Cover, then cook on low within 3 hours till casserole is set.
5. Turn off your slow cooker and let it sit within 5 minutes before serving. Optionally dust with powdered sugar (icing sugar) before serving.

Nutritional Values:

- Calories: 500
- Net Carbs: 61g
- Fat: 25g
- Protein: 15g
- Sugar: 17g

Difficulty: 1 **2** 3 4 5

Southwest Chicken Breakfast Burritos

20 min   4 hrs   6

Ingredients:

- 500g no bones & skin chicken breasts
- 250ml salsa
- 100g canned black beans, strained & washed
- 100g canned sweetcorn, strained & washed
- One green bell pepper, diced
- One onion, diced
- Two cloves minced garlic
- Salt & pepper, as required
- Six big flour tortillas, warmed
- 150g Cheddar cheese, grated
- Optional toppings: avocado, sour cream, hot sauce

Directions:

1. Put chicken breasts in your slow cooker. Put salsa, black beans, sweetcorn, green bell pepper, onion, and garlic on top. Flavour it using salt plus pepper.
2. Cover your slow cooker, then cook on low within four hours till chicken is cooked through. Once cooked, shred chicken in your slow cooker. Mix everything together.
3. Assemble your burritos by placing a heaping spoonful of chicken mixture onto the centre of each tortilla.
4. Top with grated Cheddar cheese and any additional desired toppings. Fold your tortilla sides, then then roll it up to secure all ingredients inside. Serve.

Nutritional Values:

- Calories: 518
- Net Carbs: 55g
- Fat: 16g
- Protein: 37g
- Sugar: 6g

Difficulty: 1 **2** 3 4 5

Sausage and Egg Casserole

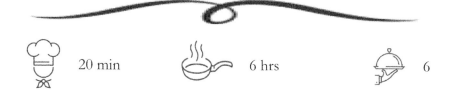

🧑‍🍳 20 min   🍳 6 hrs   🍽 6

Ingredients:

- 450g pork sausages
- One big chopped onion
- Two cloves minced garlic
- 800g canned diced tomatoes
- 240ml chicken stock
- 200g frozen mixed vegetables

- 15ml Worcestershire sauce
- 1g dried thyme
- Salt & pepper, as required
- 6 large eggs
- Chopped fresh parsley for garnish

Directions:

1. Cook the sausages on moderate temp in your pan till browned. Remove, slice, then put aside.
2. Cook the onions in your same pan till soften. Put garlic, then cook within one minute.
3. Add canned tomatoes, chicken stock, Worcestershire sauce, thyme, salt, and pepper to your slow cooker. Stir well.
4. Add cooked sausages and frozen mixed vegetables. Mix everything together. Cook within five hours on low.
5. Crack one egg at a time into your small container, then carefully slide it onto the top of the casserole mixture, keeping the yolks intact. Repeat with the remaining eggs.
6. Cook on low within an additional hour till eggs are cooked. Sprinkle with chopped parsley before serving.

Nutritional Values:

- Calories: 420
- Net Carbs: 20g
- Fat: 26g
- Protein: 28g
- Sugar: 7g

Difficulty: 1 **2** 3 4 5

Peach Cobbler Oatmeal

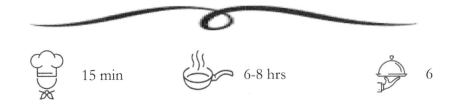

15 min   6-8 hrs   6

Ingredients:

- 200g oats, rolled
- 500ml almond milk
- 300ml water
- 30ml honey
- 5ml vanilla extract
- 1.25g salt

- 800g canned peaches, drained and chopped (or fresh peaches, if available)
- 100g light brown sugar
- 1.3g cinnamon
- 60g butter, unsalted dissolved

Directions:

1. Mix oats, milk, water, honey, vanilla, and salt in your slow cooker. Add chopped peaches on top of the oat mixture in your slow cooker.
2. In your small container, combine light brown sugar and cinnamon. Sprinkle it evenly on peaches. Drizzle butter on top.
3. Cover, then cook within six to eight hours on low till oats are tender. Gently stir everything before serving.

Nutritional Values:

- Calories: 395
- Net Carbs: 62g
- Fat: 14g
- Protein: 8g
- Sugar: 30g

Difficulty: **1** 2 3 4 5

Banana Bread Pudding

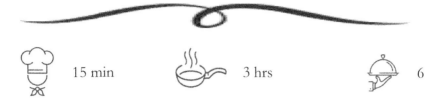

🧑‍🍳 15 min   🍳 3 hrs   🍽 6

Ingredients:

- 250g stale bread, cut into small cubes
- 100g granulated sugar
- One litre whole milk
- 500 ml heavy cream
- Four eggs
- 10ml vanilla extract
- 1.25g salt
- 2 ripe bananas, mashed
- 100g raisins or sultanas (optional)
- 50g unsalted butter, melted and cooled

Directions:

1. In your big container, mix bread cubes, sugar, mashed bananas and raisins (if using).
2. In another container, whisk milk, heavy cream, eggs, vanilla plus salt. Slowly pour it on bread mixture. Stir gently.
3. Pour melted butter into your slow cooker, then carefully pour the bread pudding mixture on top of it.
4. Cover, then cook within three hours on low till golden brown. Cool it down before serving.

Nutritional Values:

- Calories: 600
- Net Carbs: 80g
- Fat: 27g
- Protein: 14g
- Sugar: 17g

Difficulty: 1 2 3 4 5

Coconut Quinoa Porridge

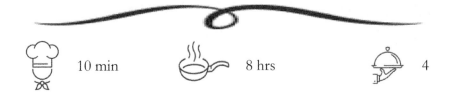

🧑‍🍳 10 min   🍳 8 hrs   🛎 4

Ingredients:

- 200g quinoa, washed & strained
- 400ml coconut milk
- 600ml water
- 30ml honey
- 5ml vanilla extract
- Salt, as required
- Toppings of choice (e.g. sliced berries, chopped nuts, or shredded coconut)

Directions:

1. Add the rinsed and drained quinoa to your slow cooker.
2. In your container, mix coconut milk, water, honey, vanilla, plus salt. Pour it over the quinoa in your slow cooker.
3. Stir well to ensure the quinoa is evenly coated with the liquid mixture. Cook for eight hours on low till porridge has reached your desired consistency.
4. Serve hot with your choice of toppings.

Nutritional Values:

- Calories: 339
- Net Carbs: 45g
- Fat: 11g
- Protein: 9g
- Sugar: 7g

Difficulty: 1 2 3 4 5

Apple Cinnamon Breakfast Risotto

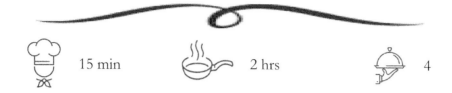

🎩 15 min   🍳 2 hrs   🍽 4

Ingredients:

- 200g Arborio rice
- One litre almond milk
- Two big apples, peeled, cored, & diced
- 75g brown sugar
- 1.3g ground cinnamon
- Salt, as required
- 25g unsalted butter
- 50g chopped walnuts
- Zest of one lemon

Directions:

1. Mix Arborio rice, milk, diced apples, sugar, ground cinnamon, and salt in your slow cooker. Cook within two hours on high till rice is tender.
2. Just before the end of cooking time, dissolve butter in your small pan on moderate temp.
3. Add chopped walnuts, then cook within three to four minutes till lightly toasted.
4. When the risotto is ready, gently stir in the buttery walnut mixture and lemon zest. Serve warm, dividing evenly among four bowls.

Nutritional Values:

- Calories: 420
- Net Carbs: 63g
- Fat: 16g
- Protein: 8g
- Sugar: 18.5g

Difficulty: 1 2 3 4 5

Pumpkin Spice Granola

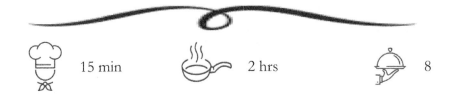

🧑‍🍳 15 min   🍳 2 hrs   🍽 8

Ingredients:

- 200g oats, rolled
- 100g pumpkin seeds
- 100g chopped pecans
- 50g dried cranberries
- 5g ground cinnamon
- 2g ground nutmeg
- 2g allspice
- 1g ground cloves
- 3g sea salt
- 120ml maple syrup
- 60ml pumpkin puree
- 50ml coconut oil, melted

Directions:

1. In your big container, mix oats, pumpkin seeds, chopped pecans, dried cranberries, cinnamon, nutmeg, allspice, cloves, and sea salt.
2. In your separate container, whisk maple syrup, pumpkin puree, and melted coconut oil. Combine with the dry mixture till blended.
3. Line your slow cooker using parchment paper. Transfer the granola mixture into your slow cooker, then spread evenly.
4. Cook within 2 hours on low with the lid slightly ajar to allow moisture to escape. Stir every 30 minutes to prevent burning and ensure even cooking.
5. After cooking, spread the granola onto a baking sheet and let it cool completely. It will crisp up as it cools. Serve.

Nutritional Values:

- Calories: 365
- Net Carbs: 45g
- Fat: 18g
- Protein: 8g
- Sugar: 20g

Difficulty: 1 **2** 3 4 5

Slow Cooker Veggie Omelette

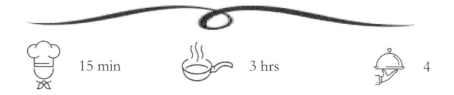

🍳 15 min   🍳 3 hrs   🍽 4

Ingredients:

- 100g chopped red bell pepper
- 100g chopped green bell pepper
- 100g chopped yellow bell pepper
- 150g mushrooms, sliced
- 50g onion, chopped
- 50g spring onions, chopped
- 150g cherry tomatoes, halved
- Eight big eggs
- 120ml milk
- Salt & pepper, as required
- 100g grated cheddar cheese

Directions:

1. Mix red, green and yellow peppers, mushrooms, onion, spring onions, and cherry tomatoes in your slow cooker.
2. In your medium container, whisk eggs and milk. Flavour it using salt plus pepper.
3. Pour it into your slow cooker over the vegetables. Sprinkle grated cheddar cheese on top.
4. Cover, then cook within three hours on low till eggs are fully set and cooked through.
5. Once cooked, let cool for a few minutes before cutting into wedges or portions to serve.

Nutritional Values:

- Calories: 312
- Net Carbs: 15g
- Fat: 21g
- Protein: 20g
- Sugar: 7g

Difficulty: **1** 2 3 4 5

Pineapple Upside Down Pancake

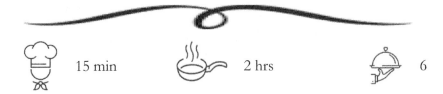

🎩 15 min   🍳 2 hrs   🛎 6

Ingredients:

- 200g self-raising flour
- 50g caster sugar
- Salt, as required
- 300ml milk
- One big egg, beaten
- 30ml vegetable oil

- 5ml vanilla extract
- 565g canned pineapple rings, drained (reserve syrup)
- Six maraschino cherries
- 100g unsalted butter, melted
- 100g dark brown sugar

Directions:

1. Mix self-raising flour, caster sugar, plus salt in your big container. Add milk, beaten egg, vegetable oil, and vanilla extract. Mix till a smooth batter forms.
2. Grease your slow cooker pot with non-stick spray or butter.
3. In your separate container, mix melted butter and dark brown sugar. Pour the brown sugar mixture into your pot.
4. Add pineapple rings on top, positioning one ring in the centre and arranging the others around it. Add a cherry in the middle of each pineapple ring.
5. Pour the pancake batter on the pineapples and cherries gently. Close, then cook for two hours on high till golden brown.
6. Let it cool slightly before flipping it onto a serving plate.

Nutritional Values:

- Calories: 510
- Net Carbs: 75g
- Fat: 20g
- Protein: 10g
- Sugar: 37g

Difficulty: 1 **2** 3 4 5

Breakfast Corned Beef Hash

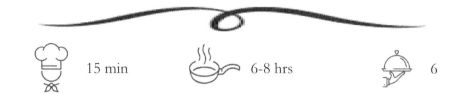

15 min   6-8 hrs   6

Ingredients:

- 500g corned beef, cubed
- 1kg potatoes, peeled and cubed
- Two big onions, chopped
- 500g carrots, peeled and sliced
- One litre beef stock
- One bay leaf
- 200g frozen peas
- Salt & pepper, as required

Directions:

1. Add cubed corned beef, potatoes, onions, and carrots in your slow cooker. Mix them well. Pour in beef stock, then add bay leaf. Stir well.
2. Close, then cook for six to eight hours on low.
3. About half an hour before serving, add the peas to your slow cooker. Mix well, then cook till peas are heated through.
4. Before serving, remove the bay leaf.
5. Flavour it using salt plus pepper.

Nutritional Values:

- Calories: 437
- Net Carbs: 38g
- Fat: 21g
- Protein: 25g
- Sugar: 5g

Difficulty: 1 **2** 3 4 5

Strawberry Cheesecake Oatmeal

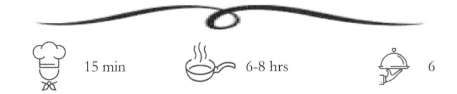

🧑‍🍳 15 min   ♨ 6-8 hrs   🍽 6

Ingredients:

- 300g rolled oats
- One litre almond milk
- 250g fresh strawberries, sliced
- 200g cream cheese, softened
- 75g granulated sugar
- 150ml water
- 5ml vanilla extract

Directions:

1. Mix rolled oats, almond milk, and half of the sliced strawberries in your slow cooker. Put aside.
2. In your container, mix cream cheese, sugar, plus vanilla. Swirl it into your oats till evenly distributed.
3. Pour water into your slow cooker to ensure that the mixture won't dry out during cooking. Cook for six to eight hours or overnight on low.
4. After cooking, give the oatmeal a good stir and top it with remaining sliced strawberries. Serve warm.

Nutritional Values:

- Calories: 357
- Net Carbs: 42g
- Fat: 16g
- Protein: 11g
- Sugar: 12g

Difficulty: 1 **2** 3 4 5

Blueberry Almond Overnight Quinoa

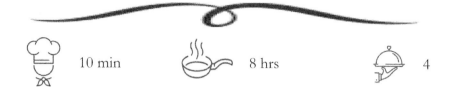

10 min   8 hrs   4

Ingredients:

- 200g quinoa, washed & strained
- 800ml almond milk
- 100g fresh blueberries
- 50g almonds, chopped
- 30ml honey
- 5ml vanilla extract
- Salt, as required

Directions:

1. Mix rinsed quinoa, milk, honey, vanilla, and salt in your slow cooker. Cover, then cook within eight hours or overnight on low.
2. In the morning, give your quinoa mixture a good stir.
3. Divide the quinoa mixture into four servings and top each with fresh blueberries and chopped almonds.

Nutritional Values:

- Calories: 380
- Net Carbs: 53g
- Fat: 13g
- Protein: 12g
- Sugar: 19g

Difficulty: **1** 2 3 4 5

Honey Garlic Chicken

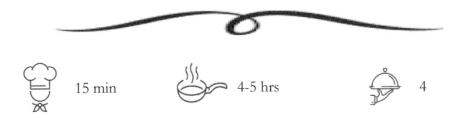

15 min   4-5 hrs   4

Ingredients:

- 600g no bones & skin chicken thighs
- 100ml honey
- 60ml light soy sauce
- 40ml ketchup
- Two cloves minced garlic

- One small onion, diced
- 8g cornflour
- 30ml water
- Salt & pepper, as required

Directions:

1. Mix honey, soy sauce, ketchup, minced garlic, and diced onion in your small container.
2. Flavour your chicken thighs using salt and pepper. Put it in your slow cooker.
3. Add honey garlic mixture on your chicken, then mix together till chicken is evenly coated.
4. Set your slow cooker to low temp, then cook for four to five hours. Check whether the chicken is cooked through.
5. When the cooking time is up, whisk cornflour and water in your small container to create a slurry. Stir this into your slow cooker to thicken the sauce.
6. Cook within 20 minutes on low temp with the lid removed. Serve.

Nutritional Values:

- Calories: 435
- Net Carbs: 31g
- Fat: 17g
- Protein: 41g
- Sugar: 27g

Difficulty: 1 2 **3** 4 5

Lemon Herb Chicken

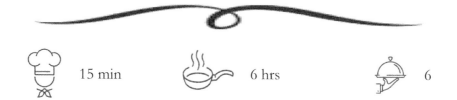

🧑‍🍳 15 min   🍳 6 hrs   🛎 6

Ingredients:

- 1.5kg skinless chicken breasts
- One big lemon, zest and juice
- Four cloves minced garlic
- 2g dried thyme
- 1.2g dried rosemary
- 250ml chicken broth
- 15ml olive oil
- Salt & pepper, as required

Directions:

1. Mix zest, lemon juice, garlic, thyme, rosemary, salt plus pepper in your small container.
2. Pour olive oil into your slow cooker, then add chicken breasts. Pour lemon herb mixture on top. Pour chicken broth around the sides of the chicken.
3. Cover, then cook within six hours on low till chicken is tender. Serve.

Nutritional Values:

- Calories: 275
- Net Carbs: 2g
- Fat: 6g
- Protein: 48g
- Sugar: 0g

Difficulty: **1** 2 3 4 5

Creamy Mushroom Chicken Thighs

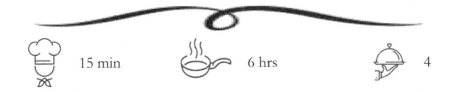

15 min   6 hrs   4

Ingredients:

- Eight (about 600g) no bones & skin chicken thighs
- 250g fresh button mushrooms, sliced
- One big white onion, finely chopped
- Three garlic cloves, minced
- 250ml chicken broth

- 200ml heavy cream
- 30ml Worcestershire sauce
- 15g mustard (Dijon or wholegrain)
- 8g cornstarch
- Salt & pepper, as required

Directions:

1. Lightly season chicken thighs using salt and pepper, then put aside.
2. In your medium-sized pan, sauté the onions and garlic within four minutes on moderate temp till soft.
3. Put onions, garlic, mushrooms, and chicken thighs into your slow cooker.
4. In your container, whisk chicken broth, Worcestershire sauce, mustard, and cornstarch till well combined. Pour it in your slow cooker. Close, then cook for six hours on low.
5. About half an hour before serving time, mix in heavy cream, then cook within thirty minutes till heated through. Serve.

Nutritional Values:

- Calories: 450
- Net Carbs: 10g
- Fat: 25g
- Protein: 45g
- Sugar: 5g

Difficulty: 1 **2** 3 4 5

Slow Cooked Teriyaki Chicken

15 min   6 hrs   4

Ingredients:

- 600g no bones & skin chicken thighs
- 120ml teriyaki sauce
- 60ml soy sauce
- 60ml honey
- Two cloves minced garlic
- 6g fresh ginger, grated
- 15g cornflour
- 60ml cold water
- Four spring onions, chopped
- Sesame seeds (optional)
- Steamed rice, to serve

Directions:

1. In your small container, whisk teriyaki & soy sauce, honey, garlic plus ginger.
2. Put chicken thighs in your slow cooker. Add sauce mixture on it. Close, then cook within six hours on low. Remove the chicken, then put it on your plate.
3. In another small container, mix corn flour and cold water till smooth. Pour it into your slow cooker, then stir gently with the remaining sauce.
4. Add cooked chicken, then cook within 15 minutes on high. Garnish cooked chicken with chopped spring onions and sesame seeds (if using).

Nutritional Values:

- Calories: 342
- Net Carbs: 24g
- Fat: 9g
- Protein: 40g
- Sugar: 17g

Difficulty: 1 2 **3** 4 5

Slow Cooked Chicken & Dumplings

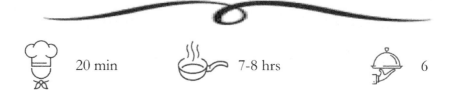

20 min   7-8 hrs   6

Ingredients:

- 800g no bones & skin chicken breasts or thighs, cubed
- One litre chicken stock
- 200g frozen mixed vegetables (carrots, peas, corn)
- One big onion, diced

- Two cloves minced garlic
- 300g self-raising flour
- 150ml milk
- 75g cold unsalted butter, cubed
- 1g dried thyme
- Salt & pepper, as required

Directions:

1. Mix cubed chicken, chicken stock, frozen mixed vegetables, diced onion, minced garlic, and dried thyme in your slow cooker. Flavour it using salt plus pepper. Cook within 6 hours on low.
2. For the dumplings, in your medium container mix together the self-raising flour plus salt. Add butter, then rub it into your flour till mixture crumbly.
3. Gradually pour milk, stirring gently with a fork till a sticky dough forms. Divide it into six, then shape into balls.
4. Place dough balls on top of the chicken mixture in your slow cooker, spacing them evenly.
5. Cook within 1-2 hours on high till dumplings have doubled in size and are cooked through. Serve.

Nutritional Values:

- Calories: 543
- Net Carbs: 47g
- Fat: 23g
- Protein: 37g
- Sugar: 4g

Difficulty: 1 2 3 **4** 5

Buffalo Chicken Mac & Cheese

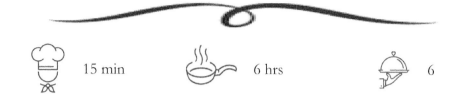

15 min   6 hrs   6

Ingredients:

- 450g no bones & skin chicken breasts
- 500g elbow macaroni
- 600ml whole milk
- One litre chicken broth
- 120g diced mozzarella cheese
- 120g grated mature cheddar cheese
- 100g buffalo hot sauce
- 50g unsalted butter
- 40g all-purpose flour
- 3g powdered garlic
- Salt & pepper, as required

Directions:

1. Put chicken breasts in your slow cooker. Pour in chicken broth, then cook within four hours on low till chicken is cooked through. Remove the chicken, shred it, then put aside.
2. In your skillet, cook the elbow macaroni as directed to package instructions till tender. Strain, then put aside.
3. In your medium saucepan, melt butter on moderate temp. Gradually whisk in the flour to form a roux. Cook within one minute, whisking continuously.
4. Slowly pour in milk, whisking constantly to create a smooth bechamel sauce. Cook within five minutes, stirring frequently till thickened.
5. Add powdered garlic, salt, plus pepper, followed by both cheeses. Stir till completely melted and fully incorporated.
6. Mix in cooked macaroni and shredded chicken till evenly coated. Transfer this mixture and buffalo hot sauce to your slow cooker. Mix well.
7. Cook within two hours on low till heated through and flavours are blended.

Nutritional Values:

- Calories: 660
- Net Carbs: 58g
- Fat: 29g
- Protein: 41g
- Sugar: 8g

Difficulty: 1 2 **3** 4 5

Turkey Chili Verde

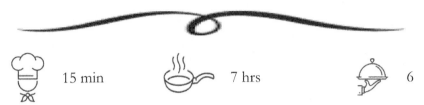

🧑‍🍳 15 min   🍳 7 hrs   🍽 6

Ingredients:

- 600g no bones & skin turkey breast, cut into chunks
- 400g tomatillos, husked & chopped
- Two medium green bell peppers, chopped
- One big onion, chopped
- Two jalapeno peppers, seeded & minced
- Three cloves minced garlic
- 500ml chicken stock
- 400g tin cannellini beans, strained & washed
- 150g frozen sweetcorn
- 40g fresh coriander leaves, chopped
- Juice of one lime (about 30ml)
- 5ml ground cumin
- Salt & pepper, as required

Directions:

1. Layer the turkey pieces in your slow cooker. Add chopped tomatillos, green bell peppers, onion, minced jalapenos, and garlic on top. Pour in chicken stock.
2. Cover, then cook within 6 hours on low. After 6 hours, remove the lid, then transfer the cooked turkey onto your plate. Cool it down before shredding.
3. Stir in the cannellini beans, sweetcorn, cumin into your slow cooker. Add the shredded turkey, then mix well.
4. Cook for another hour on low before stirring in coriander leaves and lime juice. Flavour it using salt plus pepper. Serve.

Nutritional Values:

- Calories: 320
- Net Carbs: 38g
- Fat: 3g
- Protein: 33g
- Sugar: 7g

Difficulty: 1 **2** 3 4 5

Thai Coconut Curry Chicken

🧑‍🍳 15 min   🍳 6 hrs   🍽 6

Ingredients:

- 1kg no bones & skin chicken breasts, cut into bite-sized pieces
- 400ml full-fat coconut milk
- 200ml chicken broth
- 150g red curry paste (use less for milder curry)
- 100g chopped onions
- 100g sliced each green & red bell pepper
- Four cloves minced garlic
- 30ml fish sauce
- 25g brown sugar
- Juice of one lime
- Salt & pepper, as required
- Fresh coriander leaves for garnish

Directions:

1. Mix coconut milk and chicken broth in your slow cooker. Mix in red curry paste and mix well.
2. Add the garlic, onions, along with both red and green bell peppers. Gently add the chicken pieces.
3. Add fish sauce and brown sugar to your slow cooker and gently combine everything. Cover, then cook within 6 hours on low.
4. When the cooking is complete, flavour it using salt plus pepper (if needed), then mix in lime juice. Serve.

Nutritional Values:

- Calories: 341
- Net Carbs: 17g
- Fat: 19g
- Protein: 26g
- Sugar: 7g

Difficulty: 1 **2** 3 4 5

Tuscan Chicken Stew

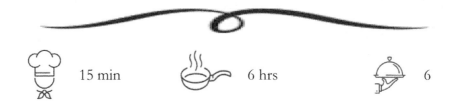

🎩 15 min   🍳 6 hrs   🍽 6

Ingredients:

- 600g no bones & skin chicken breasts, cut into chunks
- 300g baby potatoes, halved
- 100g carrots, sliced
- One chopped onion
- Four garlic minced cloves
- One red bell pepper, chopped
- 150g baby spinach
- 400g can cannellini beans, strained & washed
- 400g can diced tomatoes, with juice
- 500ml chicken broth
- 30g tomato paste
- Salt & pepper, as required
- 1.25g dried oregano
- 1g dried basil
- 55g dried rosemary

Directions:

1. Mix chicken, potatoes, carrots, onion, garlic, and bell pepper in your slow cooker.
2. In your container, mix cannellini beans, tomatoes (with juice), broth, plus tomato paste. Flavour it using salt, pepper, oregano, basil, and rosemary.
3. Pour it in your slow cooker. Cover, then cook within six hours on low till chicken is tender.
4. Add baby spinach during the last 30 minutes, then stir well to incorporate. Serve.

Nutritional Values:

- Calories: 320
- Net Carbs: 35g
- Fat: 6g
- Protein: 30g
- Sugar: 6g

Difficulty: 1 **2** 3 4 5

Moroccan Spiced Turkey Tagine

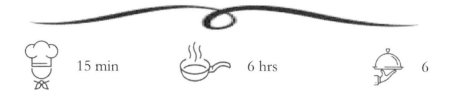

15 min   6 hrs   6

Ingredients:

- One kg diced turkey
- One big chopped onion
- Three cloves minced garlic
- Two chopped carrots, sliced
- One chopped red bell pepper
- One chopped yellow bell pepper
- 400g canned chickpeas, strained & washed
- 400g canned tomatoes, chopped
- 100g dried apricots, halved
- 500ml chicken stock
- 30g tomato paste
- 30ml honey
- 4g ground cumin
- 4g ground coriander
- 1g ground cinnamon
- Salt & ground black pepper, as required

Directions:

1. Cook the turkey in your big pan on moderate temp, till browned on all sides. Move it to your slow cooker.
2. Add onions and garlic to your pan, then cook till softened. Add spices (cumin, coriander, cinnamon), then cook within one minute before transferring to your slow cooker.
3. Mix in carrots, bell peppers, chickpeas, canned tomatoes, apricots, chicken stock, tomato paste and honey. Mix well.
4. Flavour it using salt plus ground black pepper. Cook within 6 hours on low till turkey is tender and vegetables are cooked through.
5. Before serving, adjust seasoning if necessary and garnish with fresh coriander or parsley.

Nutritional Values:

- Calories: 435
- Net Carbs: 44g
- Fat: 10g
- Protein: 42g
- Sugar: 19g

Difficulty: 1 2 **3** 4 5

Mediterranean Stuffed Turkey Breasts

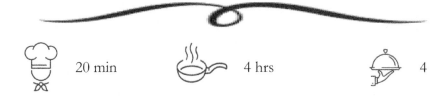

🍳 20 min 🍲 4 hrs 🍽 4

Ingredients:

- Four (about 150g each) turkey breast fillets
- 100g feta cheese, crumbled
- 50g chopped sun-dried tomatoes
- 50g pitted & sliced black olives
- Two cloves minced garlic
- 3g fresh basil, chopped
- Salt & pepper, as required
- 150ml chicken stock
- 15ml cornflour, mixed in with a little cold water

Directions:

1. Lay the turkey breasts flat on your cutting board. Make an incision along their thicker edges to make a pocket.
2. In your small container, mix feta cheese, tomatoes, olives, garlic, and basil.
3. Stuff turkey breast pockets with the Mediterranean mixture, then flavour it using salt plus pepper.
4. Place the stuffed turkey breasts into your slow cooker. Pour chicken stock along its side. Cover, then cook within three to four hours on low till cooked.
5. Carefully transfer cooked stuffed turkey breasts to a serving platter and set aside.
6. Stir in cornflour mixture into slow cooker's remaining liquid to thicken up the sauce. Pour over stuffed turkey breasts as desired before serving.

Nutritional Values:

- Calories: 385
- Net Carbs: 10g
- Fat: 18g
- Protein: 47g
- Sugar: 3g

Difficulty: 1 2 **3** 4 5

Roasted Pepper Duck Legs

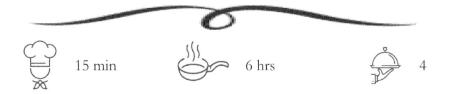

🍳 15 min   🍳 6 hrs   🛎 4

Ingredients:

- Four (about 1 kg) duck legs
- 300 ml chicken stock
- Two medium red bell peppers, sliced thinly
- One big red onion, sliced thinly
- Two garlic minced cloves
- 200 g canned chopped tomatoes
- 30ml tomato paste
- 15ml Worcestershire sauce
- 5g paprika
- 1g dried thyme
- Salt & black pepper, as required

Directions:

1. Pat the duck legs dry using paper towels, then flavour it using salt plus black pepper.
2. In your big pan on moderate temp, sear the duck legs, skin-side down within five minutes till crispy. Flip the legs, then cook for another three minutes. Remove, then put aside.
3. In your same pan, add bell peppers and onions. Cook within five minutes till softened. Then add minced garlic, then cook within one minute.
4. In your slow cooker, mix together the cooked vegetables, chopped tomatoes, tomato paste, Worcestershire sauce, paprika, thyme and chicken stock.
5. Submerge the duck legs into the vegetable mixture.
6. Cook within 6 hours on low till duck legs are tender and easily pull apart with a fork. Serve.

Nutritional Values:

- Calories: 465
- Net Carbs: 15g
- Fat: 29g
- Protein: 34g
- Sugar: 8g

Difficulty: 1 2 **3** 4 5

Garlic Parmesan Chicken Wings

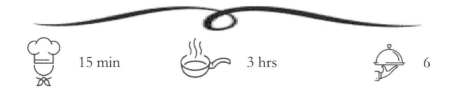

15 min   3 hrs   6

Ingredients:

- 1.5kg chicken wings
- 60ml olive oil
- 30g grated Parmesan cheese
- Four cloves minced garlic
- 15ml Worcestershire sauce

- 2g basil, dried
- 2g oregano, dried
- Salt & black pepper, as required

Directions:

1. In your small container, mix olive oil, grated Parmesan cheese, garlic, Worcestershire, basil, oregano, salt, and black pepper.
2. Put chicken wings in your slow cooker, then pour sauce mixture on top. Toss well. Cook for 3 hours on low till tender.
3. Warm up your oven to grill setting or 200°C. Line your baking tray using foil.
4. Carefully transfer the cooked chicken wings from your slow cooker to the lined tray using tongs. Grill within 5 minutes till slightly crispy. Serve.

Nutritional Values:

- Calories: 440
- Net Carbs: 2g
- Fat: 33g
- Protein: 34g
- Sugar: 0g

Difficulty: 1 **2** 3 4 5

Country-Style Duck Ragu

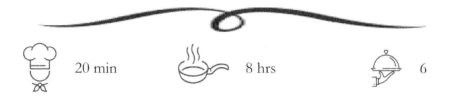

🍳 20 min   🍳 8 hrs   🍽 6

Ingredients:

- 1.5kg duck legs (with skin on)
- 30ml olive oil
- Two onions, finely chopped
- Two cloves minced garlic
- One diced medium carrot
- One diced celery stalk
- 400g canned chopped tomatoes
- 200ml dry white wine
- 500ml chicken stock
- One litre tomato passata (sieved tomatoes)
- Two bay leaves
- Salt & pepper, as required

Directions:

1. Warm up olive oil in your skillet on moderate temp. Add duck legs, then cook within five minutes on each side till crispy. Remove the duck legs, then put aside.
2. In your same skillet, cook the onions, garlic, carrot, and celery within five minutes till softened.
3. Transfer the cooked vegetables to your slow cooker. Add canned chopped tomatoes, dry white wine, chicken stock, tomato passata, and bay leaves.
4. Put browned duck legs on top. Cover, then cook within eight hours on low.
5. After cooking, remove the duck legs from your slow cooker and carefully remove the tender meat from the bones. Discard any bones or skin.
6. Return shredded duck meat to slow cooker and mix into sauce. Flavour it using salt plus pepper. Serve.

Nutritional Values:

- Calories: 632
- Net Carbs: 23g
- Fat: 42g
- Protein: 39g
- Sugar: 12g

Difficulty: 1 2 **3** 4 5

Orange Glazed Cornish Hen

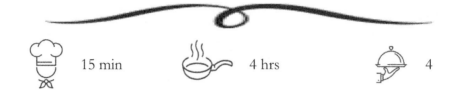

🍳 15 min   🍲 4 hrs   🍽 4

Ingredients:

- Two (approx. 900g each) Cornish hens, giblets and excess fat removed & pat dried
- Salt & pepper, as required
- 120ml orange marmalade
- 60ml soy sauce
- 60ml orange juice
- 15ml honey
- Two cloves minced garlic
- 5g fresh ginger, grated
- Zest of one orange

Directions:

1. Flavour the hens using salt and pepper, then place them in your slow cooker.
2. In your small container, mix orange marmalade, soy sauce, orange juice, honey, garlic, ginger and orange zest. Stir well to make the sauce.
3. Pour it evenly over the hens. Cover, then cook within 4 hours on low till cooked.
4. Remove the cooked hens from your slow cooker and transfer to a serving plate. Drizzle remaining sauce from slow cooker over Cornish hens. Serve.

Nutritional Values:

- Calories: 450
- Net Carbs: 28g
- Fat: 24g
- Protein: 31g
- Sugar: 21g

Difficulty: 1 **2** 3 4 5

Pork Tenderloin with Apples

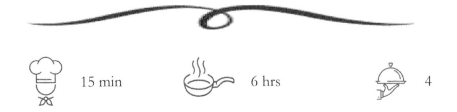

15 min   6 hrs   4

Ingredients:

- 600g pork tenderloin
- Four cored & chopped medium apples
- One chopped big onion
- Two cloves minced garlic
- 250ml dry white wine
- 150ml chicken broth
- 30g Dijon mustard
- 8g cornstarch
- Salt & pepper, as required

Directions:

1. Add the chopped apples and onions in your slow cooker. Flavour the pork tenderloin using salt and pepper, then put it on top.
2. Mix garlic, white wine, chicken broth, and Dijon mustard in your small container. Pour this mixture over the tenderloin.
3. Cover, then cook within 6 hours on low till tender. Remove the tenderloin, then cool it down before slicing.
4. Pour the remaining juices into your saucepan.
5. In your medium container, mix the cornstarch and enough water to create a smooth paste. Add this to your saucepan and whisk till thickened on moderate temp.
6. Serve slices of pork with apples and onions, topped with the thickened sauce from your slow cooker.

Nutritional Values:

- Calories: 400
- Net Carbs: 28g
- Fat: 10g
- Protein: 45g
- Sugar: 18g

Difficulty: 1 2 **3** 4 5

BBQ Beef Brisket in Red Wine Sauce

🧑‍🍳 20 min   🍳 8 hrs   🍽 6

Ingredients:

- 1.5kg beef brisket
- 30ml vegetable oil
- Two sliced big onions
- Four minced garlic cloves
- 500ml red wine
- 250ml beef stock
- 400g canned chopped tomatoes
- 80g mixed dried fruit (such as raisins and currants)
- 30ml Worcestershire sauce
- 5g paprika
- 8g brown sugar
- Salt & pepper, as required

Directions:

1. Warm up vegetable oil in your big pan on moderate-high temp. Sear the brisket till browned, then move it to your slow cooker.
2. In your same pan, add onions, then cook till tender. Put garlic, then cook within one minute.
3. Mix in red wine, scraping up any browned bits. Simmer within a few minutes to reduce slightly.
4. Mix in beef stock, chopped tomatoes, Worcestershire sauce, mixed dried fruit, paprika, brown sugar, salt, plus pepper.
5. Pour it on the brisket. Cover, then cook within 8 hours on low till brisket is cooked.
6. Move the brisket to your cutting board, cool it down, then slice against the grain.
7. Meanwhile, skim off any excess fat on your sauce in your slow cooker, then spoon it over the sliced brisket. Serve.

Nutritional Values:

- Calories: 622
- Net Carbs: 29g
- Fat: 20g
- Protein: 72g
- Sugar: 22g

Difficulty: 1 2 **3** 4 5

Moroccan Spiced Lamb Stew

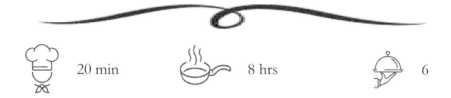

🧑‍🍳 20 min   🍳 8 hrs   🍽 6

Ingredients:

- 800g lamb shoulder, trimmed and cubed
- One big onion, chopped
- Three cloves minced garlic
- One litre vegetable stock
- 400g can diced tomatoes
- 100g dried apricots, chopped
- 400g can chickpeas, strained & washed
- Two peeled & chopped big carrots
- 200g peeled & chopped sweet potatoes
- 50g raisins
- 15ml olive oil
- 5g ground cumin
- 5g ground coriander
- 3g ground cinnamon
- 1g ground ginger
- Salt & pepper, as required

Directions:

1. Warm up olive oil in your big pan on moderate temp. Put onion plus garlic, then cook within four minutes till softened.
2. Put lamb cubes, then brown within five minutes. Transfer it to your slow cooker.
3. Stir in the vegetable stock, tomatoes, apricots, chickpeas, carrots, sweet potatoes, raisins, cumin, coriander, cinnamon, and ginger to your slow cooker.
4. Cook within 8 hours on low till lamb is cooked through. Flavour it using salt plus pepper. Serve.

Nutritional Values:

- Calories: 485
- Net Carbs: 38g
- Fat: 22g
- Protein: 34g
- Sugar: 18g

Difficulty: 1 **2** 3 4 5

Maple Glazed Pork Ribs

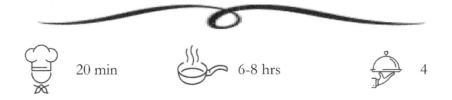

🧑‍🍳 20 min   🍳 6-8 hrs   🍽️ 4

Ingredients:

- 1kg pork ribs
- 200ml pure maple syrup
- 100ml apple cider vinegar
- 50ml Worcestershire sauce
- 50g brown sugar
- 14g smoked paprika

- 30g Dijon mustard
- 8g powdered garlic
- 7g powdered onion
- Salt & pepper, as required

Directions:

1. In your container, mix maple syrup, vinegar, Worcestershire, brown sugar, smoked paprika, Dijon, powdered garlic, powdered onion, salt, plus pepper to create the glaze.
2. Lay the pork ribs side by side in your slow cooker. Pour the glaze evenly over the ribs. Cook within six to eight hours on low till meat is cooked. Serve.

Nutritional Values:

- Calories: 650
- Net Carbs: 35g
- Fat: 41g
- Protein: 32g
- Sugar: 27g

Difficulty: 1 **2** 3 4 5

Beef and Mushroom Stroganoff

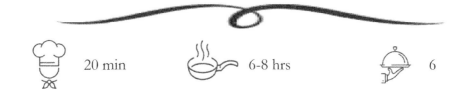

20 min   6-8 hrs   6

Ingredients:

- 800g beef chuck, sliced into cubes
- 200g sliced mushrooms
- One chopped big onion
- Two cloves minced garlic
- 250ml beef stock
- 250g sour cream

- 30ml Worcestershire sauce
- 5g Dijon mustard
- Salt & pepper, as required
- 30ml vegetable oil
- 150ml white wine (optional)

Directions:

1. In your big pan, warm up vegetable oil on moderate temp. Add the beef cubes and brown them evenly. Once browned, transfer the beef to your slow cooker.
2. Add garlic, onions, plus mushrooms to your pan, then cook till softened. Transfer it to your slow cooker.
3. In your container, mix beef stock, Worcestershire, Dijon mustard, salt, and pepper. Pour it into your slow cooker. If using wine, add it at this step.
4. Cover, then cook within six to eight hours on low till meat is tender. Mix in sour cream till combined well with the sauce before serving.
5. Serve your stroganoff over rice or noodles.

Nutritional Values:

- Calories: 410
- Net Carbs: 9g
- Fat: 28g
- Protein: 31g
- Sugar: 3g

Difficulty: 1 2 **3** 4 5

Mediterranean Lamb Shanks with Olives

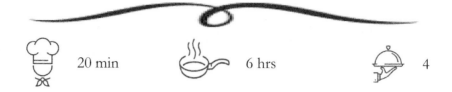

20 min   6 hrs   4

Ingredients:

- Four lamb shanks (approximately 1kg total)
- One chopped big onion
- Two cloves minced garlic
- One (400g) can chopped tomatoes
- 200g Kalamata olives, pitted
- 30g tomato paste
- 250ml chicken or vegetable stock
- 2 sprigs fresh rosemary
- Zest of one lemon
- Salt & pepper, as required

Directions:

1. Flavour the lamb shanks using salt plus pepper. Brown them in your frying pan on moderate-high temp till all sides are seared. Transfer browned shanks to your slow cooker.
2. In your same frying pan, cook onions plus garlic within 5 minutes, tilly soften. Then add the tomatoes, tomato paste, and chicken stock. Stir well, then let it boil.
3. Slowly pour it on the lamb shanks in your slow cooker. Add the rosemary sprigs on top. Cover, then cook within 6 hours on low till meat is tender.
4. About an hour before serving, add the Kalamata olives and lemon zest to your slow cooker, stirring gently to incorporate them.
5. Once cooked, carefully transfer lamb shanks onto a serving dish. Ladle sauce from slow cooker over top of them to keep them moist.

Nutritional Values:

- Calories: 648
- Net Carbs: 18g
- Fat: 41g
- Protein: 54g
- Sugar: 6g

Difficulty: 1 2 **3** 4 5

Teriyaki Pork and Pineapple Stir Fry

🧑‍🍳 15 min   🍳 4 hrs   🍽 4

Ingredients:

- 500g boneless pork shoulder, sliced
- 250g pineapple, cubed
- One sliced each green & red bell pepper
- One chopped onion
- Two garlic minced cloves
- 80ml teriyaki sauce
- 60ml pineapple juice

- 30ml soy sauce
- 15ml honey
- 10g cornstarch
- 3g ground ginger
- Salt & pepper, as required

Directions:

1. Place sliced pork shoulder, pineapple, peppers, and onion in your slow cooker.
2. In your small container, mix together teriyaki sauce, pineapple juice, soy sauce, honey, garlic and ground ginger. Pour it on pork shoulder mixture. Flavour it using salt plus pepper.
3. Cook within 4 hours on low till pork is tender.
4. Before serving, thicken the sauce by whisking cornstarch with some water in small bowl; add it to your slow cooker and stir well. Cook within 5-10 minutes till slightly thickened. Serve.

Nutritional Values:

- Calories: 450
- Net Carbs: 40g
- Fat: 12g
- Protein: 46g
- Sugar: 28g

Difficulty: 1 **2** 3 4 5

Cuban Mojo Pulled Pork Sandwiches

Ingredients: 30 min   8 hrs   8

- 1.5kg boneless pork shoulder, trimmed of excess fat
- 15ml olive oil
- 120ml orange juice
- 60ml lime juice

- 60ml lemon juice
- Five garlic minced cloves
- One sliced big onion
- 2g dried oregano
- 1g ground cumin

- Salt & pepper, as required
- Olive oil, for browning the meat
- Eight crusty bread rolls or baguettes

For the mojo sauce:

- 120ml olive oil
- Four garlic minced cloves
- Salt & pepper, as required
- Zest & juice of one lemon and one lime

Directions:

1. In your small container, mix all juices, garlic, oregano, and ground cumin. Put aside. Flavour the pork shoulder using salt plus pepper.
2. Warm up 15ml olive oil in your big skillet on moderate-high temp. Sear the pork till evenly browned.
3. Place the sliced onion in your slow cooker. Put seared pork on top. Pour the prepared citrus juice mixture over the pork. Cook within eight hours on low till pork is cooked. Remove, then shred it.
4. Strain the cooking liquid in a saucepan to make mojo sauce by separating solids from liquids—discard solids.
5. Add olive oil and minced garlic to cooking liquid, season with salt, pepper, lemon zest & lime zest & heat for a few minutes. Pour half of warm mojo sauce on the shredded pork and mix well. Reserve the remaining mojo sauce for serving.
6. Toast bread rolls or baguettes, fill each with a generous portion of pulled pork, and drizzle with reserved mojo sauce.

Nutritional Values:

- Calories: 610
- Net Carbs: 35g
- Fat: 35g
- Protein: 43g
- Sugar: 6g

Difficulty: 1 2 3 **4** 5

Balsamic Marinated Beef Pot Roast

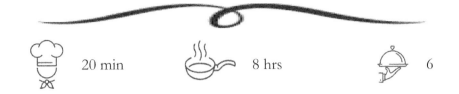

🍳 20 min   🍲 8 hrs   🍽 6

Ingredients:

- 1.5kg beef pot roast
- 250ml balsamic vinegar
- 250ml red wine
- 500ml beef broth
- Two sliced big onions
- Two cloves minced garlic
- Three medium-sized carrots, chopped
- Three medium-sized potatoes, cubed
- 30ml Worcestershire sauce
- 15ml olive oil
- Salt & pepper, as required

Directions:

1. In your small container, mix balsamic vinegar, Worcestershire sauce, salt and pepper.
2. Pour it on the beef pot roast in a shallow dish, ensuring that it is evenly coated. Cover, then refrigerate within two hours.
3. In your pan on moderate temp, warm up the olive oil, then cook the beef pot roast till browned.
4. Place half of sliced onions in your slow cooker, followed by browned beef, potatoes, and carrots.
5. Add minced garlic to your pan used for browning the beef, then cook for one minute. Deglaze with red wine and cook within two minutes.
6. Pour wine and garlic mixture over the beef in your slow cooker, followed by beef broth to cover ingredients sufficiently.
7. Cook within eight hours on low till meat is cooked but not falling apart. Serve.

Nutritional Values:

- Calories: 600
- Net Carbs: 20g
- Fat: 28g
- Protein: 60g
- Sugar: 8g

Difficulty: 1 2 **3** 4 5

Indian-Spiced Lamb Curry

20 min   6-8 hrs   6

Ingredients:

- 1kg lamb, diced
- Two big onions, chopped
- Four cloves minced garlic
- One thumb-sized piece ginger, grated
- 2 tbsp vegetable oil
- 400 g canned diced tomatoes
- 4g garam masala

- 2g ground cumin
- 2g ground coriander
- 3g ground turmeric
- 2g red chili powder (or to taste)
- 400 ml coconut milk
- Salt & pepper, as required

Directions:

1. Warm up vegetable oil in your big skillet on moderate temp, then cook the onions within eight minutes till softened. the garlic and ginger, cooking within one minute. Add the lamb, then cook till browned.
2. In your separate container, mix canned tomatoes with garam masala, ground cumin, coriander, turmeric, and red chili powder.
3. Transfer the cooked onion-lamb mixture to your slow cooker. Pour the spiced tomato mixture on the lamb; stir well to coat completely.
4. Cook within six to eight hours on low till lamb is tender and flavours have melded together.
5. Thirty minutes prior to serving, remove the lid from your slow cooker and stir in coconut milk; allow to cook uncovered for a thicker curry sauce. Flavour it using salt plus pepper. Serve.

Nutritional Values:

- Calories: 534
- Net Carbs: 13g
- Fat: 41g
- Protein: 29g
- Sugar: 4g

Difficulty: 1 2 **3** 4 5

Bourbon Brown Sugar Glazed Ham

🧑‍🍳 15 min   🍳 8 hrs   🛎 12

Ingredients:

- One (4 kg) bone-in spiral-sliced ham
- 150ml bourbon whiskey
- 250g dark brown sugar
- 80ml maple syrup
- 100ml Dijon mustard
- Ten whole cloves
- 250ml water

Directions:

1. Place the spiral-sliced ham in your big slow cooker, cut-side down.
2. In your medium container, mix together the bourbon, dark brown sugar, maple syrup, and Dijon mustard. Pour this mixture on the ham. Stud the top of the ham with whole cloves, evenly spaced.
3. Pour the water around the base of the ham to ensure it doesn't dry out during cooking.
4. Cover, then cook within 8 hours on low, basting occasionally with cooking juices.
5. After the cooking time is complete, transfer the ham to your cutting board.
6. If desired, thicken remaining juices into a glaze by transferring them to a saucepan and simmering on medium-low temp till desired consistency is reached.
7. Slice the ham and drizzle with glaze before serving.

Nutritional Values:

- Calories: 525
- Net Carbs: 28g
- Fat: 25g
- Protein: 47g
- Sugar: 27g

Difficulty: 1 2 **3** 4 5

Beef and Vegetable Chili

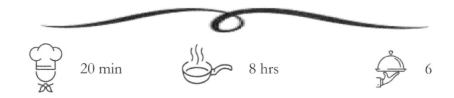

20 min   8 hrs   6

Ingredients:

- 500g lean beef, diced
- 300g mixed bell peppers, chopped
- 200g onions, chopped
- 150g carrots, chopped
- 400g canned red kidney beans, strained & washed
- 400g canned chopped tomatoes
- 250ml beef stock
- Two cloves minced garlic
- 15ml vegetable oil
- 14g chili powder
- 2g ground cumin
- Salt & pepper, as required

Directions:

1. Warm up vegetable oil in your pan on moderate temp. Add diced beef, then cook till browned.
2. Transfer the browned beef to your slow cooker. Add bell peppers, onions, carrots, plus minced garlic.
3. In your container, mix chili powder, ground cumin, and canned tomatoes. Pour it on the beef.
4. Add red kidney beans and beef stock to your slow cooker. Stir to combine all ingredients.
5. Close, then cook within 8 hours on low till beef is cooked.
6. Flavour it using salt plus pepper. Serve.

Nutritional Values:

- Calories: 290
- Net Carbs: 28g
- Fat: 8g
- Protein: 24g
- Sugar: 5g

Difficulty: 1 **2** 3 4 5

Rosemary Garlic Leg of Lamb

20 min   8 hrs   6

Ingredients:

- 2kg leg of lamb, bone-in
- Four cloves minced garlic
- Two sprigs fresh rosemary, chopped
- 250ml red wine
- 250ml beef or lamb stock

- Four medium carrots, chopped
- Two medium onions, chopped
- Salt & black pepper, as required
- 15ml olive oil

Directions:

1. In your small container, mix minced garlic and chopped rosemary. Put aside. Flavour the leg of lamb using salt and black pepper.
2. Warm up olive oil in your big pan on moderate-high temp. Sear the lamb till browned.
3. Transfer the seared lamb to a slow cooker. Rub the garlic and rosemary mixture all over the surface of the meat.
4. Add carrots and onions, nestling them around the leg of lamb. Pour in the red wine and beef or lamb stock.
5. Cover, then cook within eight hours on low till meat is cooked. Remove the leg of lamb, then cool it down before slicing.
6. Serve with carrots, onions, and some juice from your slow cooker.

Nutritional Values:

- Calories: 560
- Net Carbs: 13g
- Fat: 33g
- Protein: 52g
- Sugar: 5g

Difficulty: 1 2 **3** 4 5

Hungarian Beef Goulash

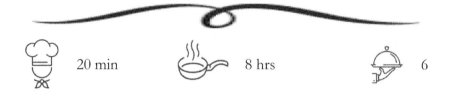

20 min   8 hrs   6

Ingredients:

- 1kg beef chuck, cubed
- 30ml vegetable oil
- Two chopped onions
- Two cloves minced garlic
- 400g canned chopped tomatoes

- 300ml beef broth
- 15g paprika
- Salt & pepper, as required
- One chopped each red & green bell pepper

Directions:

1. In your big skillet on moderate temp, warm up vegetable oil. Add the beef cubes, then cook till browned. Move it to your slow cooker.
2. In your same skillet, cook the onions and garlic within five minutes till softened. Add this mixture to your slow cooker.
3. Pour in the chopped tomatoes plus beef broth. Mix in paprika, salt plus pepper. Cover, then cook within seven hours on low.
4. After the seven hours have passed, add the chopped green and red bell peppers to your slow cooker. Cook within one hour.

Nutritional Values:

- Calories: 484
- Net Carbs: 15g
- Fat: 28g
- Protein: 40g
- Sugar: 7g

Difficulty: 1 2 **3** 4 5

Korean BBQ Beef Short Ribs

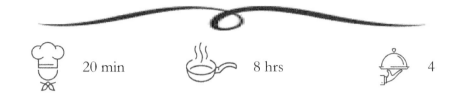

20 min   8 hrs   4

Ingredients:

- 1kg beef short ribs, cut into individual ribs
- 120ml soy sauce
- 60ml mirin (Japanese sweet rice wine)
- 60ml water
- Three cloves minced garlic
- One chopped small onion
- 50g brown sugar
- 10g gochujang (Korean hot pepper paste)
- 30ml toasted sesame oil
- Salt & pepper, as required

Directions:

1. In your container, mix soy sauce, mirin, water, minced garlic, chopped onion, brown sugar, gochujang, and toasted sesame oil. Mix well till fully blended.
2. Flavour the beef short ribs using salt plus pepper. Place them in your slow cooker.
3. Pour the sauce mixture on the ribs. Cook within eight hours on low till ribs are cooked. Remove the ribs, then transfer them to your serving plate.

Nutritional Values:

- Calories: 520
- Net Carbs: 18g
- Fat: 32g
- Protein: 37g
- Sugar: 12g

Difficulty: 1 **2** 3 4 5

Poached Cod with Fennel

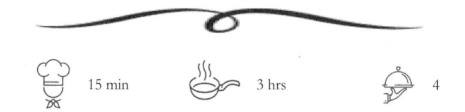

15 min   3 hrs   4

Ingredients:

- Four (150g each) cod fillets
- Two (500g) fennel bulbs, thinly sliced
- One litre vegetable broth
- 200ml white wine
- One lemon, sliced
- Two bay leaves
- Salt & pepper, as required
- Fresh dill, for garnish

Directions:

7. Arrange the thinly sliced fennel bulbs in your slow cooker. Put the cod fillets on top.
8. In your container, mix the vegetable broth and white wine together, then pour the mixture over the cod fillets and fennel.
9. Add lemon slices and bay leaves to your slow cooker, gently pushing them into the liquid. Flavour it using salt plus pepper.
10. Cover, then cook for 3 hours on low till cod is cooked through.
11. Serve each fillet with fennel slices on a plate, spooning some of the poaching liquid over the top if desired. Garnish with fresh dill.

Nutritional Values:

- Calories: 240
- Net Carbs: 10g
- Fat: 2g
- Protein: 35g
- Sugar: 0g

Difficulty: 1 2 **3** 4 5

Creamy Tuscan Salmon

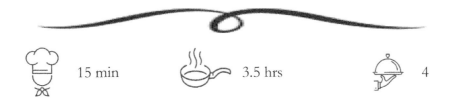

🍳 15 min   🍳 3.5 hrs   🍽 4

Ingredients:

- 800g salmon fillets
- 250ml chicken broth
- 120g sundried tomatoes, chopped
- 200g fresh spinach
- Three cloves minced garlic
- One big onion, chopped
- 400ml heavy cream
- 100g parmesan cheese, grated
- Salt & pepper, as required

Directions:

1. Place the salmon fillets in your slow cooker.
2. In your container, mix chicken broth, sundried tomatoes, minced garlic, and chopped onion together. Pour this mixture on the salmon.
3. Cover, then cook within three hours on low. Carefully remove the salmon fillets, then put them aside on your serving plate.
4. Add fresh spinach to your remaining liquid in your slow cooker, then cook for ten minutes till spinach wilts.
5. Mix in heavy cream and parmesan cheese, then continue cooking for five more minutes till heated through and combined well. Flavour it using salt plus pepper.
6. Pour creamy sauce over salmon fillets on your serving plate.

Nutritional Values:

- Calories: 729
- Net Carbs: 22g
- Fat: 51g
- Protein: 46g
- Sugar: 6g

Difficulty: 1 **2** 3 4 5

Asian Glazed Mahi Mahi

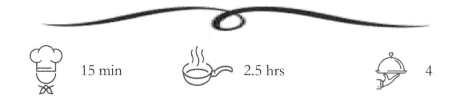

🧑‍🍳 15 min   🍳 2.5 hrs   🍽 4

Ingredients:

- Four (150g each) Mahi Mahi fillets
- 80ml soy sauce
- 80ml maple syrup
- 60ml rice vinegar
- 30g brown sugar
- One garlic minced clove
- 2cm fresh ginger, grated
- 1g red pepper flakes
- 15g cornstarch
- 45ml cold water
- Freshly chopped spring onions, for garnish
- Sesame seeds, for garnish

Directions:

1. In your medium container, whisk soy sauce, maple syrup, rice vinegar, brown sugar, minced garlic, grated ginger, and red pepper flakes.
2. Place the Mahi Mahi fillets into your slow cooker and evenly pour the sauce mixture. Cover, then cook for 2 hours on low till fish flakes easily.
3. Carefully transfer the cooked Mahi Mahi fillets to your plate and keep warm.
4. Pour the cooking sauce into your small saucepan, then simmer on moderate temp.
5. In your small container, combine the cornstarch plus cold water till slurry.
6. Slowly add cornstarch slurry, mixing till thickened to your desired consistency.
7. Plate the Mahi Mahi fillets and generously drizzle each piece with the thickened glaze.
8. Garnish with freshly chopped spring onions and sesame seeds before serving.

Nutritional Values:

- Calories: 349
- Net Carbs: 34g
- Fat: 4g
- Protein: 42g
- Sugar: 28g

Difficulty: 1 2 3 4 5

Cajun-Style Red Beans and Catfish

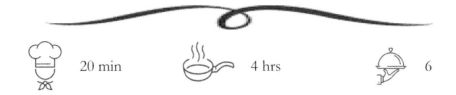

20 min   4 hrs   6

Ingredients:

- 450g dried red kidney beans, soaked overnight and drained
- One litre water
- One big chopped onion
- One chopped green bell pepper
- Three chopped celery stalks
- Four garlic minced cloves

- Two bay leaves
- 1g dried thyme
- 2g cayenne pepper
- 7g smoked paprika
- Salt & black pepper, as required
- 800g catfish fillets, cut into bite-sized pieces

Directions:

1. Mix soaked and drained kidney beans, water, onion, green bell pepper, celery stalks, garlic cloves, bay leaves, dried thyme, cayenne pepper, paprika, salt, plus pepper in your slow cooker.
2. Cook within 3.5 hours on high till beans are tender.
3. Once done, gently stir in the catfish pieces. Cover, then cook within 30 minutes till catfish flakes easily. Discard bay leaves before serving.

Nutritional Values:

- Calories: 420
- Net Carbs: 52g
- Fat: 12g
- Protein: 32g
- Sugar: 4g

Difficulty: 1 **2** 3 4 5

Clam Chowder with Potatoes

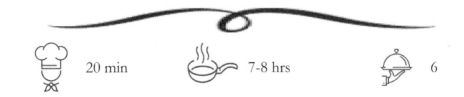

20 min   7-8 hrs   6

Ingredients:

- 500g fresh clams, cleaned & scrubbed
- 500g potatoes, peeled & chopped
- One big diced onion
- Two diced celery stalks
- One diced big carrot
- Two garlic minced cloves

- One litre vegetable broth
- 300ml whole milk or cream
- 20g all-purpose flour
- 30ml unsalted butter, melted
- Salt & pepper, as required

Directions:

1. Put cleaned clams in your slow cooker. Add the potatoes, onion, celery, carrot, and garlic. Pour the vegetable broth on top.
2. In your container, whisk milk/cream, flour, and melted butter till smooth. Stir it into your slow cooker. Flavour it using salt plus pepper.
3. Cover, then cook within seven to eight hours on low till potatoes are fork-tender.
4. About 30 minutes before serving, remove the clams (discard any that do not open) and take off their shells.
5. Slice the clam meat, then return them to your slow cooker. Stir gently. Serve.

Nutritional Values:

- Calories: 350
- Net Carbs: 42g
- Fat: 12g
- Protein: 19g
- Sugar: 4g

Difficulty: 1 **2** 3 4 5

Southern Seafood Grits

🧑‍🍳 30 min   🍳 7-8 hrs   🍽 6

Ingredients:

- 250g quick-cooking grits
- One litre chicken broth
- 150ml whole milk
- 100g unsalted butter, divided
- 5g salt
- 1g black pepper
- 300g prawns, peeled and deveined
- 300g crabmeat, flaked

- 200g cod, cut into large chunks
- 150g chopped onion
- 10g minced cloves garlic
- 150g chopped bell pepper
- 250ml tomato sauce
- 30ml Worcestershire sauce
- Fresh parsley, chopped (for garnish)

Directions:

1. Mix grits, chicken broth, milk, half of the butter (50g), salt, plus black pepper in your slow cooker. Cook within six hours on low.
2. Dissolve the remaining butter in your big skillet on moderate temp. Add onion, then cook within five minutes till softened.
3. Add garlic plus bell pepper, then cook within three minutes.
4. Mix in prawns, crabmeat, plus cod into your skillet. Cook till seafood is cooked through and opaque in colour, approximately 8 to10 minutes.
5. Stir in the tomato sauce, Worcestershire sauce, and hot sauce (if using) into the seafood mixture. Cook within one minute while stirring to combine flavours.
6. Move seafood mixture to your slow cooker. Mix well, then cook within another hour on low. Serve hot with a garnish of chopped parsley.

Nutritional Values:

- Calories: 570
- Net Carbs: 48g
- Fat: 24g
- Protein: 40g
- Sugar: 4g

Difficulty: 1 2 **3** 4 5

Lemon Garlic Herb Shrimp

15 min   1.5 hrs   4

Ingredients:

- 600g peeled & deveined shrimp
- Three cloves minced garlic
- Zest and juice of 2 lemons
- 15g parsley, fresh, chopped
- 15g basil, fresh, chopped
- 15g chives, fresh, chopped
- Salt & pepper, as required

Directions:

1. In your slow cooker, combine the minced garlic, zest, lemon juice, parsley, basil, and chives.
2. Add shrimp to your slow cooker, then gently mix with the herb mixture ensuring all shrimp are coated.
3. Cover, then cook for 1 hour and 30 minutes on low till shrimp turn pink. Taste and adjust seasoning using salt plus pepper. Serve.

Nutritional Values:

- Calories: 215
- Net Carbs: 6g
- Fat: 3g
- Protein: 33g
- Sugar: 1g

Difficulty: 1 **2** 3 4 5

Seafood Gumbo with Sausage

30 min   6 hrs   6

Ingredients:

- 500g mixed seafood (prawns, mussels, and white fish)
- 250g smoked sausage, sliced
- One chopped big onion
- Two chopped celery stalks
- One chopped each red & green bell pepper
- Three cloves minced garlic
- 800ml tomato passata
- 500ml chicken or fish stock
- 120ml white wine
- 30ml Worcestershire sauce
- 14g Creole seasoning
- Salt & black pepper, as required
- 2 sprigs of fresh thyme
- 300g long-grain white rice

Directions:

1. Combine the mixed seafood, smoked sausage, onion, celery, bell peppers, garlic, tomato passata, chicken or fish stock, white wine, Worcestershire sauce, Creole seasoning, and thyme sprigs in your slow cooker.
2. Stir well, then flavour it using salt plus black pepper. Cover, then cook within six hours on low till vegetables are tender.
3. About an hour before serving time, cook the long-grain white rice according to package instructions. Serve the seafood gumbo over a bed of steamed rice.

Nutritional Values:

- Calories: 420
- Net Carbs: 42g
- Fat: 15g
- Protein: 34g
- Sugar: 4g

Difficulty: 1 **2** 3 4 5

Tomato Shrimp Scampi

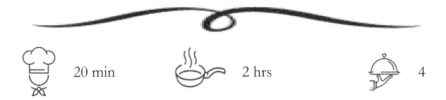

20 min   2 hrs   4

Ingredients:

- 500g peeled & deveined large shrimp
- 400g cherry tomatoes, halved
- One chopped large onion
- Three garlic minced cloves
- 150ml dry white wine
- 100ml vegetable broth
- 30ml olive oil
- Juice & zest of one lemon
- Salt & pepper, as required

Directions:

1. In your big pan, warm up olive oil on moderate temp. Add onions, then cook for five minutes till softened. Add garlic, then cook within one minute.
2. Mix in white wine and vegetable broth, then let it simmer. Move onion mixture to your slow cooker.
3. Add cherry tomatoes, lemon zest, and lemon juice. Flavour it using salt plus pepper.
4. Cook within 1 hour and 30 minutes on high. Add the shrimp, then mix well. Cook within 30 minutes on high till shrimp is cooked through. Serve.

Nutritional Values:

- Calories: 292
- Net Carbs: 10g
- Fat: 8g
- Protein: 32g
- Sugar: 6g

Difficulty: 1 **2** 3 4 5

Crockpot Shrimp Jambalaya

🧑‍🍳 15 min   🍳 7-8 hrs   🛎 6

Ingredients:

- 400g raw shrimp, peeled and deveined
- 200g skinless chicken breasts, diced
- 100g chorizo sausage, sliced
- One chopped large onion
- Two garlic minced cloves
- One chopped each green & red bell pepper

- 400g canned diced tomatoes
- 500ml chicken stock
- 150g long-grain rice, rinsed and drained
- 2g paprika
- 1g cayenne pepper
- Salt & black pepper, as required

Directions:

1. Combine shrimp, chicken, chorizo, onion, garlic, red and green bell peppers in your slow cooker.
2. Add canned diced tomatoes with their juice and chicken stock to your slow cooker.
3. Mix in the rice, paprika, cayenne pepper, salt and black pepper.
4. Cover, then cook within 7-8 hours on low till rice is tender. Stir occasionally to prevent sticking. Once cooked, serve hot with bread or a side salad.

Nutritional Values:

- Calories: 340
- Net Carbs: 30g
- Fat: 12g
- Protein: 27g
- Sugar: 6g

Difficulty: 1 **2** 3 4 5

Creamy Garlic Mashed Potatoes

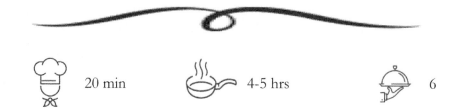

20 min   4-5 hrs   6

Ingredients:

- 1.5kg potatoes, peeled & quartered
- 240ml chicken or vegetable broth
- 120ml cream
- 80 grams unsalted butter, cut into chunks
- Six garlic minced cloves
- 15ml olive oil
- Salt & pepper, as required

Directions:

1. Place the peeled and quartered potatoes in your slow cooker. Add the chicken broth, ensuring the potatoes are submerged.
2. Cook for four to five hours on high till potatoes are fork-tender. Strain.
3. About 30 minutes before the potatoes are done, heat a pan with olive oil on moderate temp, then cook minced garlic for 2 to 3 minutes till fragrant. Put aside.
4. Mash the cooked potatoes, stirring in the butter and cream gradually till fully incorporated and silky smooth.
5. Stir in sautéed garlic, then flavour it using salt plus pepper. Serve.

Nutritional Values:

- Calories: 314
- Net Carbs: 38g
- Fat: 15g
- Protein: 5g
- Sugar: 2g

Difficulty: 1 2 **3** 4 5

Sweet Potato and Chickpea Curry

20 min   4-6 hrs   6

Ingredients:

- 1kg sweet potatoes, peeled & cut into cubes
- 400g canned chickpeas, strained & washed
- One chopped large onion
- Three cloves minced garlic
- One thumb-sized ginger, grated
- 400ml vegetable stock
- 400g canned tomatoes, crushed
- One (400ml) can coconut milk
- 30g mild curry paste
- 15g tomato paste
- Juice of half a lime
- Salt & pepper, as required

Directions:

1. Warm up your big frying pan on moderate-high temp and add oil. Add onions, garlic, and ginger, then cook within five minutes till softened.
2. Mix in curry paste and tomato paste, then cook within one minute.
3. Move onion mixture to your slow cooker, put sweet potatoes, chickpeas, vegetable stock, and crushed tomatoes.
4. Cover, then cook within four to six hours on low till sweet potatoes are tender.
5. Mix in coconut milk and lime juice, then flavour it using salt plus pepper. Serve.

Nutritional Values:

- Calories: 145
- Net Carbs: 62g
- Fat: 18g
- Protein: 10g
- Sugar: 15g

Difficulty: 1 2 **3** 4 5

Slow Cooked Ratatouille

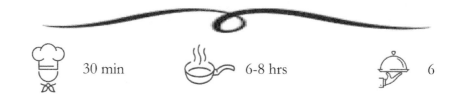

30 min   6-8 hrs   6

Ingredients:

- 500g sliced into rounds aubergine
- 500g sliced into rounds courgette
- Two sliced each yellow & red bell peppers
- One large red onion, thinly sliced
- Three garlic minced cloves
- 800g canned chopped tomatoes
- 400g cherry tomatoes, halved
- 4g dried mixed herbs (herbes de Provence)
- salt & ground black pepper, as required
- 30ml olive oil

Directions:

1. Layer the aubergine slices in your slow cooker. Add a layer of courgette slices over the aubergine. Continue with layers of bell peppers, then red onion slices and garlic.
2. Pour the canned chopped tomatoes over the vegetables. Add the cherry tomatoes on top. Sprinkle with dried mixed herbs, salt, plus black pepper.
3. Drizzle using olive oil, then gently mix. Cover, then cook within six to eight hours on low till vegetables are tender. Serve.

Nutritional Values:

- Calories: 190
- Net Carbs: 28g
- Fat: 7g
- Protein: 5g
- Sugar: 15g

Difficulty: 1 2 **3** 4 5

Zucchini Lasagna Roll-ups

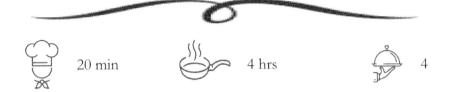

20 min   4 hrs   4

Ingredients:

- Four medium zucchinis (600g), thinly sliced lengthwise & pat dried
- 500g ricotta cheese
- 200g mozzarella cheese, shredded
- 50g Parmesan cheese, grated
- One big egg
- 15g fresh basil, chopped
- 5g dried oregano
- Salt & pepper, as required
- 500ml tomato passata (puréed tomatoes)
- 125ml vegetable stock

Directions:

1. In your big container, mix ricotta, half of the mozzarella, Parmesan cheese, egg, basil, oregano, salt, and pepper.
2. Spread about one tablespoon of cheese mixture onto each zucchini slice, then roll up tightly. Set rolled zucchinis aside.
3. In your slow cooker pot, mix tomato passata and vegetable stock together. Spread a thin layer of this mixture in your slow cooker.
4. Place rolled zucchinis seam-side down in your slow cooker pot, on top of the sauce. Pack them tightly together.
5. Pour remaining tomato passata mixture over the zucchini roll-ups and sprinkle with remaining mozzarella cheese.
6. Cover, then cook within 4 hours on low till zucchini is tender but not mushy.
7. Once cooked, carefully remove zucchini roll-ups from slow cooker using tongs or a spatula. Serve.

Nutritional Values:

- Calories: 487
- Net Carbs: 27g
- Fat: 31g
- Protein: 29g
- Sugar: 14g

Difficulty: 1 2 3 **4** 5

Collard Greens with Ham Hocks

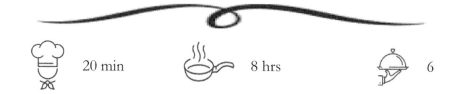

🧑‍🍳 20 min   ♨ 8 hrs   🍽 6

Ingredients:

- 500g collard greens, washed and chopped
- Two ham hocks (approximately 1kg)
- One litre chicken broth
- One big onion, chopped
- Three garlic minced cloves

- 13g brown sugar
- 2g red pepper flakes, crushed
- Salt & pepper, as required
- 30 ml apple cider vinegar

Directions:

1. Place the ham hocks on your big slow cooker. Add the collard greens, onion, garlic, brown sugar, pepper flakes, salt plus pepper.
2. Pour in broth and apple cider vinegar over the greens. Cook within 8 hours on low till ham hocks are tender and the greens are fully cooked.
3. Remove the ham hocks from your slow cooker and let them cool slightly before pulling off the meat. Discard any bones, skin or fat.
4. Shred the meat and return it to your slow cooker. Stir everything together. Serve.

Nutritional Values:

- Calories: 350
- Net Carbs: 12g
- Fat: 20g
- Protein: 30g
- Sugar: 4g

Difficulty: 1 **2** 3 4 5

Scrumptious Eggplant Parmesan

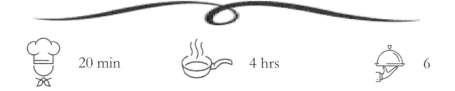

20 min   4 hrs   6

Ingredients:

- Two big eggplants, sliced into 1 cm thick rounds (about 800g)
- 400g passata
- 300g mozzarella cheese, shredded

- 150g Parmesan cheese, grated
- 100g plain flour
- Two big eggs, beaten
- Salt & black pepper, as required

Directions:

1. In your shallow container, put the flour, then flavour it using salt plus pepper. Dip each eggplant slice into the beaten eggs, then coat using the seasoned flour.
2. Layer 100ml passata in your slow cooker. Arrange a layer of eggplant slices over the passata in your slow cooker.
3. Spread another thin layer of passata (about 100ml) on top, then sprinkle with a third of both the mozzarella and Parmesan cheese.
4. Repeat this process for two more layers, ending with a layer of cheese on top. Cover, then cook within 4 hours on low till eggplant is tender and cooked through.
5. Before serving, let it sit for around 10 minutes to allow it to set.

Nutritional Values:

- Calories: 400
- Net Carbs: 30g
- Fat: 22g
- Protein: 25g
- Sugar: 10g

Difficulty: 1 2 **3** 4 5

Hearty Vegetable Pot Pie

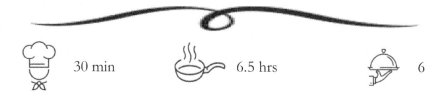

🧑‍🍳 30 min   🍳 6.5 hrs   🍽 6

Ingredients:

- 400g potatoes, cubed
- 300g carrots, sliced
- 200g parsnips, sliced
- 200g mushrooms, quartered
- 200g frozen peas
- One chopped big onion
- Two cloves minced garlic
- One litre vegetable stock
- 500ml water
- 30g tomato paste
- 15g all-purpose flour
- 30ml olive oil
- Salt & pepper, as required
- 200g self-raising flour
- 100g cold unsalted butter, diced
- Salt, as required
- Approx. 60ml cold water

Directions:

1. Mix potatoes, carrots, parsnips, mushrooms, frozen peas, and onion Iin your slow cooker.
2. In your small container or jug, whisk together the vegetable stock and tomato paste. Pour it over the vegetables. Add the minced garlic, then flavour it using salt plus pepper. Cook for 5 hours on low.
3. In your separate pan, warm up olive oil on moderate temp and whisk in the all-purpose flour.
4. Cook within two minutes while whisking, then slowly add the water while continuing to whisk till smooth.
5. Stir flour mixture into the vegetable pot pie filling and continue to cook within one hour on low till vegetables are tender. Warm up your oven to 200°C (180°C fan).
6. Make the crust by placing self-raising flour plus salt in your container. Put diced butter, then rub in till it resembles breadcrumbs.
7. Gradually add cold water, mixing till dough comes together. Roll out the dough on your floured surface to fit the top of your oven-proof dish.
8. Pour the vegetable pot pie filling into the oven-proof dish, then carefully place your rolled-out crust on top. Trim any excess dough, then press down the edges. Slice a few small slits in the crust to let steam escape. Bake within thirty minutes till crust becomes golden brown.

Nutritional Values:

- Calories: 550
- Net Carbs: 70g
- Fat: 25g
- Protein: 12g
- Sugar: 9g

Difficulty: 1 2 **3** 4 5

Slow Cooker Stuffed Bell Peppers

20 min   4-6 hrs   6

Ingredients:

- Six big bell peppers, sliced tops & seeded
- 500g lean minced beef
- 200g cooked white rice
- One chopped medium onion
- Two cloves minced garlic
- One (400g) can of chopped tomatoes
- 150ml tomato sauce
- 1g basil, dried
- 1.5g oregano, dried
- Salt & pepper, as required
- 100g grated cheddar cheese

Directions:

1. In your big container, mix minced beef, cooked rice, onion, garlic, half of canned tomatoes, half of tomato sauce, basil, oregano, salt, and pepper.
2. Fill each bell pepper with beef mixture, then top with cheddar cheese. Pour the remaining chopped tomatoes and tomato sauce into your slow cooker.
3. Put stuffed bell peppers upright in on top of tomato mixture.
4. Cook within four to six hours on low till peppers are tender. Carefully remove each pepper from your slow cooker using tongs or a slotted spoon. Serve warm.

Nutritional Values:

- Calories: 390
- Net Carbs: 36g
- Fat: 15g
- Protein: 27g
- Sugar: 9g

Difficulty: 1 2 **3** 4 5

Curried Cauliflower and Chickpeas

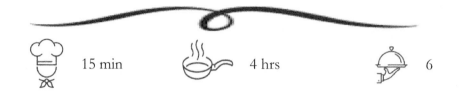

🧑‍🍳 15 min   ♨️ 4 hrs   🍽️ 6

Ingredients:

- One big cauliflower (approximately 800g), sliced into florets
- 400g canned chickpeas, rinsed and drained
- 400ml coconut milk
- 200g canned diced tomatoes
- 150g frozen peas, thawed
- One big onion, diced
- Two cloves minced garlic
- 14g curry powder
- 3g garam masala
- 3g turmeric powder
- Salt & pepper, as required
- Fresh coriander, for garnishing

Directions:

1. Mix cauliflower florets and chickpeas in your slow cooker.
2. In your container, mix the coconut milk, canned tomatoes, onion, garlic, curry powder, garam masala, and turmeric powder.
3. Pour coconut milk mixture over cauliflower and chickpeas. Cover, then cook within four hours on low till cauliflower is tender.
4. Mix in thawed peas, then flavour it using salt plus pepper. Cook for another 15 minutes on high temp till peas are heated through. Serve hot with a garnish of fresh coriander.

Nutritional Values:

- Calories: 298
- Net Carbs: 31g
- Fat: 15g
- Protein: 10g
- Sugar: 9g

Difficulty: 1 **2** 3 4 5

Root Vegetable Tagine

20 min   6 hrs   6

Ingredients:

- 500g sweet potatoes, peeled & sliced into chunks
- 400g parsnips, peeled & sliced into chunks
- 300g carrots, peeled & sliced into chunks
- 100g shallots, chopped
- Two cloves minced garlic
- 1.5 litre vegetable stock
- 400g canned chickpeas, strained & washed
- 450g canned diced tomatoes
- 100g dried apricots, chopped
- 15ml sunflower oil
- 5g ground cumin
- 5g ground coriander
- 2.5g ground cinnamon
- Salt & pepper, as required
- Fresh coriander leaves, for garnish

Directions:

1. In your big frying pan, warm up sunflower oil on moderate temp. Put shallots plus garlic, then cook within 3 minutes till softened.
2. Put cumin, coriander, plus cinnamon to the pan with shallots and garlic. Stir till fragrant, about 1 minute.
3. Transfer the seasoned shallots and garlic to your slow cooker.
4. Add sweet potatoes, parsnips, carrots, vegetable stock, chickpeas, diced tomatoes, and dried apricots to your slow cooker. Stir well.
5. Flavour it using salt plus pepper. Cover, then cook within 6 hours on low till vegetables are tender.
6. Once cooked, serve in bowls garnished with fresh coriander leaves.

Nutritional Values:

- Calories: 340
- Net Carbs: 68g
- Fat: 5g
- Protein: 9g
- Sugar: 18g

Difficulty: 1 2 **3** 4 5

Chicken & Wild Rice Soup

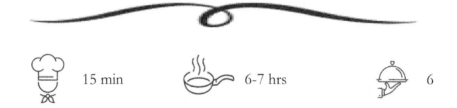

15 min   6-7 hrs   6

Ingredients:

- 400g no bones & skin chicken breast
- 100g wild rice (uncooked)
- One litre chicken stock
- 200ml water
- Two medium carrots, chopped (approx. 150g)
- Two celery stalks, chopped (approx. 100g)
- One medium onion, finely chopped (approx. 150g)
- Two garlic cloves, minced
- 2g fresh thyme leaves
- Salt & pepper, as required

Directions:

1. Put the chicken breasts in your slow cooker. Add wild rice, chicken stock, water, carrots, celery, onion, garlic, and thyme leaves. Flavour it using salt plus pepper.
2. Cover, then cook within 6 to 7 hours on low till chicken is cooked through. Remove the chicken, then shred it.
3. Add it to your slow cooker, then mix well. Serve.

Nutritional Values:

- Calories: 275
- Net Carbs: 25g
- Fat: 5g
- Protein: 30g
- Sugar: 4g

Difficulty: 1 **2** 3 4 5

Easy Tomato & Basil Soup

🧑‍🍳 10 min   🍳 6 hrs   🍽 6

Ingredients:

- One kg tomatoes, halved
- One big chopped onion
- Two cloves minced garlic
- 30g fresh basil, chopped
- One litre vegetable stock
- 250ml heavy cream
- Salt & pepper, as required
- Optional garnish: extra basil leaves

Directions:

1. Place the halved tomatoes, chopped onion, minced garlic, and chopped basil in your slow cooker. Pour the vegetable stock on top. Flavour it using salt plus pepper.
2. Cook within 6 hours on low till tomatoes are soft and cooked through. Puree the soup till smooth using your immersion blender.
3. Stir in the heavy cream till well combined. Adjust seasonings if necessary and serve hot with a garnish of extra basil leaves.

Nutritional Values:

- Calories: 204
- Net Carbs: 16g
- Fat: 14g
- Protein: 4g
- Sugar: 10g

Difficulty: 1 **2** 3 4 5

Chicken Tortilla Soup

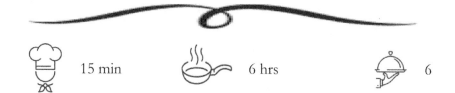

🍳 15 min   🍳 6 hrs   🍽 6

Ingredients:

- 400g no bones & skin chicken breasts
- 800ml chicken stock
- 400g tin of chopped tomatoes
- 500ml water
- 150g frozen sweetcorn

- 400g tin of black beans, strained & washed
- One big chopped onion
- Two cloves minced garlic
- One chopped red bell pepper

- One chopped green bell pepper
- Juice of one lime
- 10g chilli powder
- 5g ground cumin
- Salt & ground black pepper, as required

For garnishing:

- Fresh coriander leaves, chopped
- Crushed tortilla chips
- Grated cheddar cheese

Directions:

1. Put the chicken breasts in your slow cooker.
2. Add chicken stock, chopped tomatoes, water, sweetcorn, black beans, onion, garlic, bell peppers and jalapeño to your slow cooker.
3. Flavour it using lime juice, chilli powder, cumin, salt and pepper. Cook within 6 hours on low till chicken is cooked through.
4. Remove the chicken breasts, then shred it. Return it to your slow cooker, then mix well.
5. Serve hot in bowls with desired toppings: a sprinkle of fresh coriander leaves, crushed tortilla chips and grated cheddar cheese.

Nutritional Values:

- Calories: 365
- Net Carbs: 36g
- Fat: 8g
- Protein: 34g
- Sugar: 6g

Difficulty: 1 2 **3** 4 5

Split Pea and Ham Soup

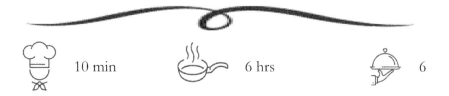

🧑‍🍳 10 min   🍳 6 hrs   🍽 6

Ingredients:

- 500g dried split peas, rinsed & drained
- 450g ham hock
- One litre chicken stock
- 500ml water
- Three medium carrots, peeled & diced
- Two diced celery stalks
- One big chopped onion
- Two cloves minced garlic
- One bay leaf
- Salt & pepper, as required

Directions:

1. Place the rinsed split peas at the bottom of your slow cooker. Add ham hock, carrots, celery, onion, and garlic on top.
2. Add chicken stock and water to cover the ingredients. Add bay leaf, salt, and pepper.
3. Cover, then cook within eight hours on low till peas are tender and ham is easily shredded.
4. Once cooked, remove the ham hock from your slow cooker and shred the meat using a fork. Discard any bones or fat.
5. Stir in shredded ham back into the soup and mix well. Remove bay leaf before serving. Adjust salt and pepper.

Nutritional Values:

- Calories: 412
- Net Carbs: 46g
- Fat: 10g
- Protein: 32g
- Sugar: 8g

Difficulty: 1 **2** 3 4 5

Thai Red Curry Vegetable Soup

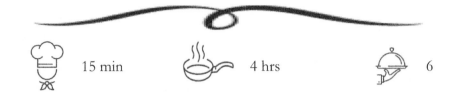

🧑‍🍳 15 min   🍳 4 hrs   🍽️ 6

Ingredients:

- 200g carrots, chopped
- 200g bell peppers, chopped
- 200g cauliflower, chopped
- 200g courgettes, chopped
- 150g baby corn, halved
- 100g mange tout, sliced
- 400ml coconut milk
- One litre vegetable broth
- 45g Thai red curry paste
- Juice of one lime
- 15ml soy sauce
- 15ml fish sauce (optional for non-vegetarians)

Directions:

1. Combine carrots, bell peppers, cauliflower, courgettes, baby corn, and mange tout in a slow cooker.
2. In your container, mix coconut milk and Thai red curry paste till smooth. Pour the coconut milk mixture on the vegetables.
3. Add the vegetable broth, then mix well. Cook for 4 hours on low. Mix in lime juice, soy sauce and fish sauce (if using) to the soup before serving.

Nutritional Values:

- Calories: 210
- Net Carbs: 20g
- Fat: 12g
- Protein: 4g
- Sugar: 9g

Difficulty: 1 **2** 3 4 5

French Onion Soup

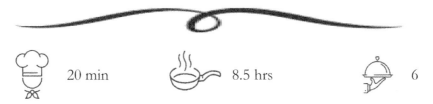

🍳 20 min   🍲 8.5 hrs   🍽 6

Ingredients:

- 1kg yellow onions, thinly sliced
- 60g unsalted butter, cubed
- 30ml olive oil
- 15g granulated sugar
- One litre beef broth
- 250ml dry white wine
- Three garlic minced cloves

- 5g fresh thyme leaves
- Two bay leaves
- Salt & black pepper, as required
- 150g Gruyère cheese, grated
- Twelve slices of baguette, toasted

Directions:

1. In your big pan on moderate temp, combine onions, butter, and olive oil. Sauté within 15 minutes till onions are soft and golden brown.
2. Add sugar, then cook for 5 minutes till onions are caramelized.
3. Transfer caramelized onions to your slow cooker. Add beef broth, white wine, garlic, thyme, bay leaves, salt, and black pepper. Mix well.
4. Cover, then cook within eight hours on low. Prior to serving, preheat your oven to broil setting on high.
5. Remove and discard the bay leaves. Ladle the soup into oven-safe bowls or ramekins.
6. Top each with two toasted baguette slices and a generous portion of grated Gruyère cheese.
7. Put the bowls under your broiler for 2-3 minutes till cheese is melted. Serve.

Nutritional Values:

- Calories: 475
- Net Carbs: 43g
- Fat: 21g
- Protein: 20g
- Sugar: 15g

Difficulty: 1 2 **3** 4 5

Italian Wedding Soup

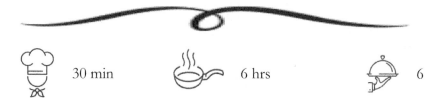

🍳 30 min　　🍲 6 hrs　　🍽 6

Ingredients:

- 250g ground pork
- 250g ground beef
- 60g fresh breadcrumbs
- 30g grated Parmesan cheese
- One egg, beaten
- Two cloves minced garlic
- Salt & pepper, as required

- One medium chopped onion
- Two carrots, sliced into rounds
- Two celery stalks, chopped
- 200g baby spinach leaves, washed and drained
- 1.5 litre low-sodium chicken broth
- 150g small pasta (e.g., orzo or ditalini)

Directions:

1. In your big container, mix ground pork, ground beef, breadcrumbs, Parmesan cheese, beaten egg, minced garlic, salt and pepper.
2. Shape the mixture into small meatballs (about the size of a marble), then put aside.
3. Put chopped onion, sliced carrots and celery in your slow cooker. Gently add the meatballs on top.
4. Pour in chicken broth, then cook within 6 hours on low till meatballs are cooked through.
5. In the last hour, add the baby spinach leaves and small pasta to your slow cooker. Once cooked through, stir gently and serve hot.

Nutritional Values:

- Calories: 430
- Net Carbs: 34g
- Fat: 20g
- Protein: 30g
- Sugar: 3g

Difficulty: 1　2　**3**　4　5

Creamy Broccoli Cheddar Soup

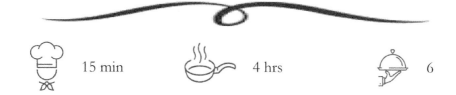

15 min   4 hrs   6

Ingredients:

- 300g fresh broccoli florets, chopped
- 200g cheddar cheese, shredded
- One litre vegetable stock
- 300ml heavy cream
- One big chopped onion
- Two cloves minced garlic

- 30g unsalted butter
- 50g plain flour
- 6g salt
- 1g black pepper

Directions:

1. In your big skillet on moderate temp, dissolve butter, then sauté the onions and garlic within 3 to 5 minutes till fragrant and tender.
2. Mix in flour, then cook within one minute to form a roux.
3. Gradually add vegetable stock to the skillet while continually stirring to avoid lumps.
4. Transfer this mixture into your slow cooker, followed by the chopped broccoli florets. Cook for 3 hours on low till broccoli is tender.
5. Blend the soup using your immersion blender till you reach your desired consistency. For a chunkier soup, only blend half of it.
6. Once blended, add the heavy cream, shredded cheddar cheese, salt, and black pepper, then mix well.
7. Cook on low within another hour to let flavours come together and cheese to fully melt. Serve.

Nutritional Values:

- Calories: 470
- Net Carbs: 19g
- Fat: 37g
- Protein: 17g
- Sugar: 5g

Difficulty: 1   2   **3**   4   5

Lamb Shank and Tomato Stew

20 min   8 hrs   4

Ingredients:

- Four lamb shanks (about 1kg total weight)
- 15ml olive oil
- One big chopped onion
- Two cloves minced garlic
- Two chopped carrots
- Two chopped celery stalks

- 400g canned chopped tomatoes
- 200ml red wine
- 250ml beef stock
- 30g tomato paste
- 15ml Worcestershire sauce
- A few sprigs of fresh rosemary and thyme
- Salt & pepper, as required

Directions:

1. In your big frying pan, warm up olive oil on moderate-high temp. Brown the lamb shanks, then move them to your slow cooker.
2. In your same pan, cook the onion within three to four minutes till softened. Add the garlic, carrots, and celery, then cook within four to five minutes.
3. Mix in chopped tomatoes, red wine, beef stock, tomato paste, and Worcestershire sauce. Add the rosemary and thyme sprigs. Flavour it using salt plus pepper.
4. Carefully pour the mixture on the lamb shanks. Cook within 8 hours on low till lamb is tender and falls off the bone.
5. Remove lamb from slow cooker carefully and serve with your choice of side dish.

Nutritional Values:

- Calories: 450
- Net Carbs: 22g
- Fat: 17g
- Protein: 45g
- Sugar: 10g

Difficulty: 1 2 **3** 4 5

Vegetable Quinoa Stew

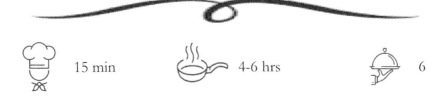

🍳 15 min　　🍳 4-6 hrs　　🍽 6

Ingredients:

- 150g quinoa, rinsed and drained
- One litre vegetable broth
- 400g canned diced tomatoes
- 400g canned cannellini beans, strained & washed
- 200g carrots, chopped
- 150g celery, chopped
- 100g onion, diced
- 150g red bell pepper, chopped
- Two cloves minced garlic
- 1g dried thyme
- 1g dried basil
- Salt & pepper, as required

Directions:

1. Mix rinsed quinoa, vegetable broth, diced tomatoes (with their juice), cannellini beans, carrots, celery, onion, red bell pepper and garlic in your slow cooker.
2. Add the dried thyme, basil, salt and pepper. Stir gently to ensure all ingredients are mixed well.
3. Cover, then cook for 4-6 hours on low till quinoa has absorbed most of the liquid. Taste and adjust seasonings as needed. Serve.

Nutritional Values:

- Calories: 254
- Net Carbs: 46g
- Fat: 3g
- Protein: 11g
- Sugar: 6g

Difficulty: 1 **2** 3 4 5

Vegan Lentil Mushroom Stew

15 min   8 hrs   6

Ingredients:

- 200g green or brown lentils, rinsed and drained
- 500g button mushrooms, cleaned and sliced
- One big chopped onion
- Two medium chopped carrots
- Three garlic minced cloves

- One litrevegetable broth
- 400g canned diced tomatoes
- 30g tomato paste
- 1g dried thyme
- 2g dried rosemary
- Salt & pepper, as required

Directions:

1. Put the lentils, mushrooms, onion, and carrots in your slow cooker.
2. Mix in minced garlic, vegetable broth, diced tomatoes, tomato paste, thyme, and rosemary.
3. Cover, then cook within 8 hours on low. After cooking time is completed, then flavour it using salt plus pepper. Mix before serving.

Nutritional Values:

- Calories: 210
- Net Carbs: 34g
- Fat: 1g
- Protein: 14g
- Sugar: 6g

Difficulty: 1 **2** 3 4 5

Seafood Cioppino Stew

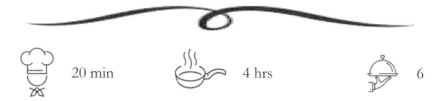

20 min   4 hrs   6

Ingredients:

- 500g mixed seafood (prawns, mussels, and squid)
- 450g diced tomatoes (canned)
- One big chopped onion
- One chopped bell pepper
- Two cloves minced garlic
- 400ml fish stock

- 200ml dry white wine
- 45ml olive oil
- 15g tomato paste
- 2g dried basil
- 1g dried oregano
- 1g red pepper flakes
- Salt & black pepper, as required

Directions:

1. In your big skillet, warm up olive oil on moderate temp. Add onion, bell pepper, and garlic. Cook within 5 minutes till onions are translucent.
2. Transfer it to your slow cooker. Add tomatoes, fish stock, white wine, tomato paste, basil, oregano plus pepper flakes. Cover, then cook within 3 hours on low.
3. After the initial cooking time of 3 hours, add the mixed seafood.
4. Cover, then continue cooking within an additional hour on low till seafood is cooked through. Flavour it using salt and black pepper. Serve.

Nutritional Values:

- Calories: 330
- Net Carbs: 15g
- Fat: 12g
- Protein: 34g
- Sugar: 6g

Difficulty: 1 **2** 3 4 5

81

Hearty Beef Stew

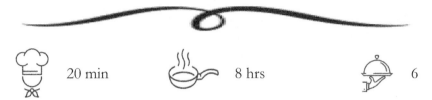

20 min   8 hrs   6

Ingredients:

- 800g sliced into cubes beef stew meat
- 300g diced potatoes
- 200g chopped carrots
- 150g chopped parsnips
- 150g chopped swede
- 150g onions, chopped
- Two cloves minced garlic

- One litre beef stock
- 500ml tomato sauce
- 45ml Worcestershire sauce
- 2g dried thyme
- Salt & pepper, as required

Directions:

1. In your pan on moderate temp, cook the beef stew meat within 5 minutes till browned. Move it into your slow cooker.
2. Add the potatoes, carrots, parsnips, swede, onions, and garlic. Pour in the beef stock, tomato sauce, and Worcestershire. Stir well to combine.
3. Flavour it using dried thyme, salt and pepper. Cook within eight hours on low till meat is tender and vegetables are cooked through. Serve.

Nutritional Values:

- Calories: 450
- Net Carbs: 35g
- Fat: 12g
- Protein: 40g
- Sugar: 9g

Difficulty: 1 **2** 3 4 5

Turkey Sausage & White Bean Stew

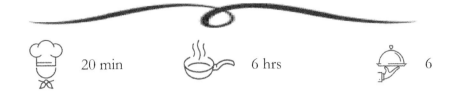

🍳 20 min   🍲 6 hrs   🍽 6

Ingredients:

- 500g turkey sausages
- 400g canned white beans, strained & washed
- 400g canned chopped tomatoes
- One litre chicken stock
- 200g carrots, sliced
- 150g celery, sliced
- One big chopped onion
- Three garlic minced cloves
- Two bay leaves
- 1g dried thyme
- Salt & pepper, as required

Directions:

1. Warm up your big skillet on moderate temp. Brown the turkey sausages within 5 minutes. Transfer to your slow cooker.
2. Mix in white beans, chopped tomatoes, chicken stock, carrots, celery, onion, garlic, bay leaves, and dried thyme. Cook within 6 hours on low.
3. Before serving, remove the bay leaves, then flavour it using salt plus pepper.

Nutritional Values:

- Calories: 320
- Net Carbs: 30g
- Fat: 8g
- Protein: 29g
- Sugar: 5g

Difficulty: 1 **2** 3 4 5

Irish Lamb and Guinness Stew

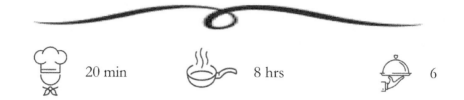

🧑‍🍳 20 min   🍳 8 hrs   🍽 6

Ingredients:

- 1kg boneless lamb shoulder, cut into 4 cm cubes
- Two big chopped onions
- Four medium carrots, peeled & sliced
- Four medium potatoes, peeled & cubed
- Two celery stalks, sliced
- Three garlic minced cloves
- 500ml Guinness stout

- 500ml beef stock
- 30g tomato paste
- 30ml Worcestershire sauce
- 1g dried thyme
- 1g dried rosemary
- Salt & pepper, as required
- Fresh parsley, finely chopped for garnishing

Directions:

1. Generously flavour lamb using salt plus pepper.
2. In your big skillet on moderate-high temp, brown lamb in batches to ensure even browning. Transfer browned lamb to your slow cooker.
3. In your same skillet, sauté onions, carrots, potatoes, celery, and garlic within 5 minutes till slightly softened. Transfer vegetables to your slow cooker.
4. In your container, mix Guinness stout, beef stock, tomato paste, Worcestershire sauce, thyme and rosemary. Pour into your slow cooker over the lamb and vegetables, then mix well.
5. Cover, then cook within 8 hours on low till lamb is tender. Flavour it using with salt and pepper.
6. Serve in deep bowls with crusty bread or mashed potatoes on the side. Garnish with fresh parsley.

Nutritional Values:

- Calories: 534
- Net Carbs: 37g
- Fat: 22g
- Protein: 34g
- Sugar: 5g

Difficulty: 1 2 **3** 4 5

Cheesy Chicken & Rice Casserole

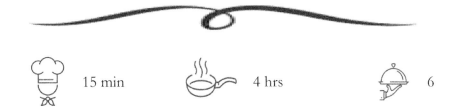

15 min   4 hrs   6

Ingredients:

- 500g no bones & skin chicken breasts, diced
- 200g long-grain white rice, uncooked
- One litre chicken broth
- 200ml milk
- 300g cheddar cheese, grated

- 100g cream cheese, softened
- One chopped onion
- Three garlic minced cloves
- 150g frozen mixed vegetables (peas, carrots, corn)
- Salt & pepper, as required

Directions:

1. In your big container, mix diced chicken breasts, uncooked rice, onion, and garlic.
2. Mix chicken broth and milk, then pour it into your slow cooker. Cook for 3 hours on low till chicken is cooked through.
3. During the last hour, mix in frozen mixed vegetables, cream cheese, and half of cheddar cheese. Flavour it using salt plus pepper.
4. Just before serving, sprinkle the remaining cheddar cheese on top and let it melt within a few minutes. Serve.

Nutritional Values:

- Calories: 550
- Net Carbs: 53g
- Fat: 22g
- Protein: 38g
- Sugar: 5g

Difficulty: 1 **2** 3 4 5

Veggie & Quinoa Casserole

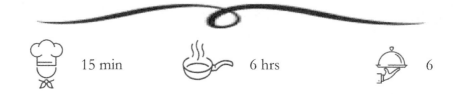

15 min   6 hrs   6

Ingredients:

- 200g quinoa
- 500ml vegetable broth
- One litre tomato passata
- One big chopped onion
- Two garlic minced cloves
- One chopped red bell pepper
- One chopped yellow bell pepper
- One courgette, sliced
- 200g mushrooms, sliced
- 250g cherry tomatoes, halved
- 100g baby spinach
- 15ml olive oil
- Salt & pepper, as required

Directions:

1. Rinse quinoa thoroughly under cold water in a fine mesh strainer and drain well. In a slow cooker, add vegetable broth and tomato passata.
2. Stir in rinsed quinoa, chopped onions, minced garlic, chopped bell peppers, sliced courgette, sliced mushrooms, and halved cherry tomatoes.
3. Drizzle olive oil on top, then flavour it using salt plus pepper. Mix well. Cook within 6 hours on low till quinoa is fully cooked but not mushy.
4. In the last half hour, stir in baby spinach and continue cooking till wilted. Serve warm.

Nutritional Values:

- Calories: 253
- Net Carbs: 42g
- Fat: 5g
- Protein: 11g
- Sugar: 9g

Difficulty: 1 2 **3** 4 5

Chicken Alfredo Tortellini Bake

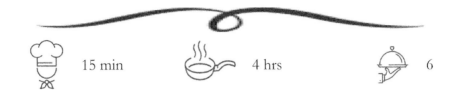

15 min   4 hrs   6

Ingredients:

- 500g no bones & skin chicken breasts
- 350g cheese tortellini (fresh or frozen)
- 450g jar of Alfredo sauce
- 250ml chicken stock
- 100g mozzarella cheese, grated

- 100g parmesan cheese, grated
- 100g fresh spinach, chopped
- Two cloves minced garlic
- Salt & pepper, as required

Directions:

1. Put chicken breasts in your slow cooker.
2. In your medium container, mix together the Alfredo sauce and chicken stock. Pour it on the chicken breasts.
3. Cook within 3.5 hours on low till chicken is fully cooked. Remove the chicken, shred it, then put aside.
4. Add the garlic, chopped spinach and cheese tortellini into the sauce in your slow cooker, stirring to combine. Add the shredded chicken, then mix well.
5. Cover, then cook within 30 minutes on low till tortellini is cooked through.
6. Sprinkle over mozzarella plus parmesan cheese, then cook within a few minutes till melted. Flavour it using salt plus pepper. Serve.

Nutritional Values:

- Calories: 550
- Net Carbs: 42g
- Fat: 28g
- Protein: 36g
- Sugar: 3g

Difficulty: 1 2 **3** 4 5

Chili Cheese Tater Tot Casserole

🧑‍🍳 20 min   🍳 6 hrs   🍽 6

Ingredients:

- 500g frozen Tater Tots
- 400g ground beef
- One medium chopped onion
- One clove minced garlic
- 400g canned kidney beans, strained & washed
- 400g canned tomatoes with juice, chopped
- 80ml tomato ketchup
- 30ml Worcestershire sauce
- One litre beef stock
- 2.5g salt
- 0.5g black pepper
- 1g chili powder
- 200g cheddar cheese, grated

Directions:

1. In your big skillet, cook the ground beef with chopped onion and garlic on moderate temp till browned. Strain any excess fat.
2. Add cooked ground beef mixture to your slow cooker along with kidney beans, canned tomatoes with juice, tomato ketchup, Worcestershire sauce, beef stock, salt, black pepper, and chili powder. Stir to combine.
3. Cover, then cook within 5 hours on low. After five hours, gently mix, then layer the frozen Tater Tots on top of the chili.
4. Cook within 1 hour on low till Tater Tots are golden brown and crisp.
5. Sprinkle the grated cheddar cheese on top, then cook within 15 minutes till cheese is melted.

Nutritional Values:

- Calories: 560
- Net Carbs: 46g
- Fat: 32g
- Protein: 29g
- Sugar: 7g

Difficulty: 1 2 **3** 4 5

Sausage, Pepper & Spinach Lasagna

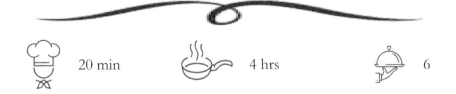

20 min   4 hrs   6

Ingredients:

- 500g pork sausages, casings removed
- One big chopped onion
- One chopped red bell pepper
- Two garlic minced cloves
- 800g canned chopped tomatoes
- 400g tomato passata
- 300g fresh spinach leaves
- 200g lasagna sheets
- 500ml béchamel sauce
- 150g grated cheddar cheese
- Salt & pepper, as required

Directions:

1. In your pan on moderate temp, cook the sausage meat with the onion and bell pepper till browned. Add garlic and cook within one minute.
2. Mix in chopped tomatoes and passata, flavour it using salt plus pepper, then let it simmer. Cook within 5 minutes to let the flavours blend together.
3. In your slow cooker, start by layering one-third of sausage mixture on the bottom. Follow with one-third of the spinach leaves and one-third of the lasagna sheets (break to fit if necessary).
4. Pour one-third of the béchamel sauce over the lasagna sheets. Repeat this process two more times to create three layers in total.
5. Top with grated cheddar cheese as you finish adding final layer. Cover, then cook within 4 hours on low till pasta is cooked through.
6. Allow it to sit within 10 minutes before serving to further set the lasagna.

Nutritional Values:

- Calories: 725
- Net Carbs: 55g
- Fat: 43g
- Protein: 33g
- Sugar: 12g

Difficulty: 1 2 3 **4** 5

Buffalo Chicken Enchilada Casserole

🧑‍🍳 20 min   🍳 4 hrs   🍽 6

Ingredients:

- 600g no bones & skin chicken breasts
- 240ml Buffalo hot sauce
- 240ml cream cheese
- 240ml sour cream
- One big chopped onion
- One diced red bell pepper
- One (400g) tin of black beans, strained & washed
- 300g tin of sweetcorn, drained
- Six big whole wheat tortillas (approximately 30cm in diameter)
- 200g grated cheddar cheese

Directions:

1. Mix chicken and Buffalo hot sauce in your slow cooker. Cook on low within approximately 3 hours or till chicken is cooked through.
2. Remove the chicken, then shred it. Put aside.
3. In your big container, mix cream cheese and sour cream till smooth. Mix in onion, red bell pepper, black beans, and sweetcorn.
4. Cut each tortilla in half. Line your slow cooker with half of the tortillas pieces, overlapping them as needed to cover the entire surface.
5. Layer half of the shredded chicken on top. Spread half of vegetable and cream cheese mixture over the chicken layer.
6. Repeat steps with the remaining tortillas, chicken, and vegetable mixture. Sprinkle the grated cheddar cheese evenly over the top layer.
7. Cover, then cook within one hour on low till all layers are heated through and cheese is fully melted. Cool it down, then serve.

Nutritional Values:

- Calories: 685
- Net Carbs: 49g
- Fat: 36g
- Protein: 42g
- Sugar: 7g

Difficulty: 1 2 3 4 5

Spinach Artichoke Ravioli Casserole

🍳 20 min   🍲 4 hrs   🍽 6

Ingredients:

- 300g frozen spinach, thawed and drained
- 200g canned artichoke hearts, drained and chopped
- One small diced onion
- Two cloves minced garlic
- 200ml Alfredo sauce
- 30g grated Parmesan cheese
- 100g cream cheese, cubed
- Salt & black pepper, as required
- 300g fresh spinach and ricotta ravioli
- 200 ml vegetable broth

Directions:

1. In your big container, combine the thawed spinach, artichoke hearts, onion, garlic, Alfredo sauce, Parmesan cheese, and cream cheese. Flavour it using salt plus pepper. Mix well.
2. In your slow cooker, spread some spinach-artichoke mixture. Then arrange a single layer of fresh spinach and ricotta ravioli on top.
3. Pour the vegetable broth evenly over the ravioli layer. Top with the rest of the spinach-artichoke mixture, making sure all the ravioli is covered by it.
4. Cover, then cook within 4 hours on low. Check to see if the ravioli is cooked through by inserting a knife into one of the pieces (it should be tender). Serve.

Nutritional Values:

- Calories: 345
- Net Carbs: 24g
- Fat: 19g
- Protein: 16g
- Sugar: 3g

Difficulty: 1 2 **3** 4 5

Crockpot Green Bean Casserole

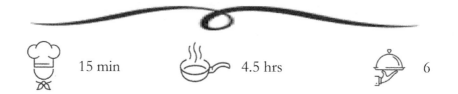

15 min   4.5 hrs   6

Ingredients:

- 700g fresh green beans, trimmed & sliced in half
- 300g cream of mushroom soup
- 150ml milk
- One chopped onion

- Two cloves minced garlic
- 120g grated cheddar cheese
- 100g French-fried onions
- Salt & pepper, as required

Directions:

1. In your big container, mix mushroom soup, milk, onion, garlic, and grated cheddar cheese. Add the green beans, then stir tilly are coated evenly.
2. Pour the green bean mixture into your slow cooker. Flavour it using salt plus pepper.
3. Cook within 4 hours on low till green beans are tender. About 20 minutes before serving, warm up your oven to 180°C.
4. Transfer the cooked green bean mixture from your slow cooker into an oven-safe casserole dish with a slotted spoon.
5. Evenly sprinkle French-fried onions on top. Bake within 25 minutes till onions are crispy. Serve.

Nutritional Values:

- Calories: 285
- Net Carbs: 20g
- Fat: 17g
- Protein: 13g
- Sugar: 4g

Difficulty: 1 **2** 3 4 5

Butternut Squash Pasta Bake

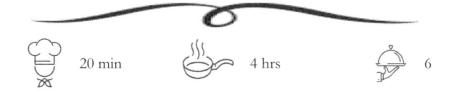

20 min   4 hrs   6

Ingredients:

- 1kg butternut squash, peeled and cubed
- 500g penne pasta
- One big chopped onion
- Two cloves minced garlic
- 150g spinach, washed and drained
- 500ml vegetable stock
- 400ml tomato passata

- 200ml double cream
- 150g grated mature Cheddar cheese
- 100g grated Parmesan cheese
- 15ml olive oil
- Salt & pepper, as required

Directions:

1. In your slow cooker, mix butternut squash, onion, garlic, spinach, vegetable stock, and tomato passata.
2. Cook within 3 hours on low till butternut squash is tender.
3. Meanwhile, in your big pot of boiling water, cook the pasta within two minutes less than the recommended time on the package to allow within additional cooking in your slow cooker. Drain and set aside.
4. After the butternut squash mixture has cooked for the required time and has become tender, add the cooked pasta to your slow cooker. Mix well.
5. Gently stir in the double cream, then flavour it using salt plus pepper. Sprinkle both Cheddar and Parmesan cheeses evenly on top.
6. Cover, then for another hour on low till cheeses are melted and bubbly. Serve.

Nutritional Values:

- Calories: 658
- Net Carbs: 90g
- Fat: 23g
- Protein: 26g
- Sugar: 11g

Difficulty: 1 2 **3** 4 5

Salsa Verde Chicken Taquitos

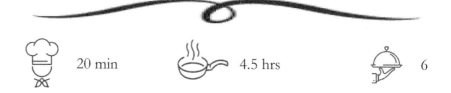

🍳 20 min   🍳 4.5 hrs   🍽 6

Ingredients:

- 600g no bones & skin chicken breasts
- 500ml salsa verde
- One big chopped onion
- Two cloves minced garlic
- 2g ground cumin

- Salt & pepper, as required
- Twelve corn tortillas (about 15cm diameter)
- 200g grated cheddar cheese
- 30ml vegetable oil

Directions:

1. Mix chicken breasts, salsa verde, chopped onion, minced garlic, ground cumin, salt, and pepper in your slow cooker.
2. Cover, then cook for 4 hours on high till chicken is easily shredded. Warm up your oven to 200°C (180° fan) gas mark 6.
3. Once the chicken is fully cooked, shred it, then mix it with the sauce in your slow cooker.
4. Warm the tortillas in a microwave within 20 seconds to make them pliable. Fill each tortilla with approximately two tablespoons of shredded chicken mixture plus a sprinkle of cheddar cheese.
5. Roll each tortilla tightly around the filling, then put seam-side down onto your baking tray.
6. Lightly brush the top of each taquito using vegetable oil. Bake within 25 minutes till crisp. Serve.

Nutritional Values:

- Calories: 515
- Net Carbs: 37g
- Fat: 25g
- Protein: 38g
- Sugar: 4g

Difficulty: 1 2 **3** 4 5

Desserts

Chocolate Lava Cake

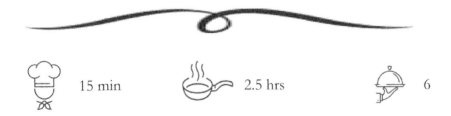

15 min   2.5 hrs   6

Ingredients:

- 200g dark chocolate, chopped
- 200g unsalted butter, cut into small pieces
- 200g granulated sugar
- Four big eggs
- 150g self-raising flour
- 50g cocoa powder
- 1.5g salt
- 125ml whole milk
- 100g milk chocolate, chopped

Directions:

1. In your microwave-safe container, mix dark chocolate and butter. Dissolve in your microwave at half power, stirring every 30 seconds till smooth.
2. In your separate container, whisk sugar and eggs till slightly thickened. Slowly pour the melted chocolate mixture into your egg mixture while whisking.
3. In another container, sift self-raising flour and cocoa powder. Add salt.
4. Add the sifted dry fixings into your chocolate and egg mixture in thirds, alternating with the milk and stirring gently after each addition till just combined. Mix in milk chocolate chunks.
5. Oil your slow cooker using non-stick cooking spray. Pour the cake batter evenly into your slow cooker.
6. Cover, then cook within 2 hours and 30 minutes on low till set around the edges but still slightly gooey in the centre.
7. Turn off your slow cooker and let cake stand within 10 minutes before serving.

Nutritional Values:

- Calories: 698
- Net Carbs: 75g
- Fat: 40g
- Protein: 12g
- Sugar: 33g

Difficulty: 1 2 3 **4** 5

Caramel Apple Crumble

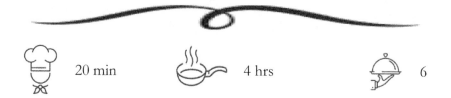

20 min   4 hrs   6

Ingredients:

- 6 apples (Granny Smith or your preferred variety), peeled, cored, and sliced
- 100g granulated sugar
- 90g unsalted butter, melted
- 180g plain flour
- 100g rolled oats

- 80g dark brown sugar
- 2.5g ground cinnamon
- 1.5g salt
- 150ml caramel sauce (store-bought or homemade)

Directions:

1. In your big container, mix sliced apples and granulated sugar. Put aside.
2. In another container, mix butter, plain flour, rolled oats, dark brown sugar, ground cinnamon, and salt. Mix till consistency is crumbly.
3. Pour the apple slices into your slow cooker and evenly distribute them at the bottom.
4. Drizzle half of the caramel sauce over the apples. Sprinkle the crumble mixture on top, evenly spreading it out.
5. Cook within 4 hours on low till crumble topping is golden brown. Remove, then cool it down.
6. Serve warm with the remaining caramel sauce drizzled over each portion.

Nutritional Values:

- Calories: 449
- Net Carbs: 82g
- Fat: 14g
- Protein: 6g
- Sugar: 27g

Difficulty: 1 2 **3** 4 5

Slow Cooked Bananas Foster

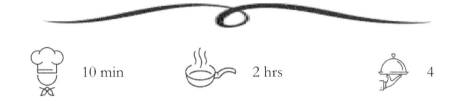

🍳 10 min   🍲 2 hrs   🍽 4

Ingredients:

- Four big ripe bananas, sliced
- 100g light brown sugar
- 50g unsalted butter, sliced into small pieces
- 2.5g cinnamon

- 0.55g nutmeg
- 30ml maple syrup
- 60ml dark rum
- 30ml banana liqueur
- 400ml vanilla ice cream, for serving

Directions:

1. In your big container, mix bananas, brown sugar, butter, cinnamon, nutmeg, and maple syrup. Toss gently to coat the bananas evenly.
2. Pour the banana mixture into your slow cooker. Cover, then cook within 2 hours on low till sauce is bubbling.
3. In your small saucepan, warm up dark rum and banana liqueur on moderate temp till warmed through. Carefully ignite the mixture using your long lighter, then let it burn off the alcohol within 15 seconds.
4. Pour the ignited rum mixture on the cooked bananas. Gently mix to incorporate into the sauce. Serve warm over scoops of vanilla ice cream.

Nutritional Values:

- Calories: 380
- Net Carbs: 58g
- Fat: 12g
- Protein: 2g
- Sugar: 25g

Difficulty: 1 2 **3** 4 5

Peanut Butter Brownies

🧑‍🍳 15 min   🍳 2 hrs   🍽 8

Ingredients:

- 200g dark chocolate, chopped
- 100g unsalted butter
- Three big eggs
- 150g caster sugar
- 5ml vanilla extract

- 150g self-raising flour
- 50g cocoa powder
- 1.5g salt
- 120g smooth peanut butter

Directions:

1. In your heatproof container, melt the dark chocolate and butter in your microwave, stirring every 30 seconds till smooth. Put aside.
2. In your big container, whisk eggs, caster sugar, and vanilla extract till creamy. Pour the chocolate mixture into your egg mixture and gently fold it in.
3. Sift the self-raising flour, cocoa powder, plus salt into your container, then fold till thoroughly mixed with no dry patches.
4. Transfer half of the brownie batter to a greased slow cooker liner. Dollop spoonfuls of peanut butter over the layer of brownie mix in your slow cooker.
5. Pour the rest of brownie batter on the peanut butter dollops, then spread evenly to cover.
6. Cook for 2 hours on high till it set. Remove, cool it down, slice, then serve.

Nutritional Values:

- Calories: 514
- Net Carbs: 52g
- Fat: 31g
- Protein: 10g
- Sugar: 18g

Difficulty: 1 2 3 4 5

Sticky Toffee Pudding

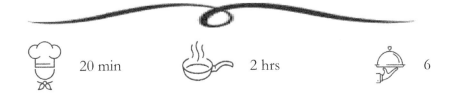

🧑‍🍳 20 min   🍳 2 hrs   🍽 6

Ingredients:

- 200g pitted dates, chopped
- 250ml boiling water
- 5ml bicarbonate of soda
- 100g unsalted butter, softened
- 150g light brown sugar
- Two big eggs
- 190g self-raising flour
- 5ml vanilla extract
- Pinch of salt

For the sauce:

- 100g unsalted butter
- 150g light brown sugar
- 200ml double cream

Directions:

1. In your heatproof container, mix chopped dates, boiling water, and bicarbonate of soda. Put aside within 5 minutes.
2. In your big container, cream the softened butter plus light brown sugar till pale and fluffy.
3. Beat in the eggs one at a time, adding a spoonful of the self-raising flour along with each egg to prevent curdling.
4. Fold in the remaining self-raising flour, vanilla extract, and salt. Mix in date mixture (including any remaining liquid) till well combined.
5. Oil your slow cooker using butter, then pour in the batter, smoothing it down evenly. Cook for 2 hours on high till it's set.
6. For the sauce, melt together unsalted butter, light brown sugar, and double cream in your saucepan on low temp till smooth.
7. Pour half sauce on the cooked pudding, then put aside to rest for a few minutes.
8. Cut servings from the pudding and serve with remaining warm toffee sauce drizzled on top.

Nutritional Values:

- Calories: 745
- Net Carbs: 82g
- Fat: 45g
- Protein: 6g
- Sugar: 32g

Difficulty: 1 2 3 **4** 5

Lemon Blueberry Cake

🍳 20 min   🍲 3 hrs   🍽 6

Ingredients:

- 200g plain flour
- 150g granulated sugar
- 10g baking powder
- 1.5g salt
- 240ml milk
- 80ml vegetable oil

- One big egg, lightly beaten
- 6g lemon zest
- Juice of one lemon (approx. 30ml)
- 150g fresh blueberries

Directions:

1. In your big container, whisk flour, sugar, baking powder, plus salt.
2. In your separate container, mix the milk, vegetable oil, egg, zest, and lemon juice. Combine it the dry mixture till blended. Gently fold in the blueberries.
3. Grease your slow cooker using some butter. Pour the cake batter into your slow cooker, then spread evenly.
4. Put your clean dish towel under the lid of your slow cooker to catch any condensation that may form and prevent it from dripping onto the cake.
5. Cook on low within 3 hours till cooked through. Turn off your slow cooker and carefully remove your slow cooker insert by holding it with oven mitts or kitchen towels – it will be hot!
6. Allow it to cool on your wire rack within 20 minutes before serving.

Nutritional Values:

- Calories: 410
- Net Carbs: 58g
- Fat: 16g
- Protein: 7g
- Sugar: 25g

Difficulty: 1 2 **3** 4 5

Apple Bread Pudding

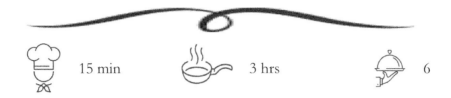

🧑‍🍳 15 min   🍳 3 hrs   🍽 6

Ingredients:

- 250g stale bread, cubed
- 100g granulated sugar
- 2.5g ground cinnamon
- Two big apples, peeled, cored and chopped
- 500ml whole milk
- 250ml double cream
- 10g unsalted butter, melted
- Two big eggs, beaten
- 5ml vanilla extract

Directions:

1. Mix stale bread cubes, granulated sugar, ground cinnamon, and chopped apples in your big container.
2. In your separate container, whisk milk, double cream, butter, beaten eggs, and vanilla extract.
3. Pour the wet mixture on the bread and apple mixture, then gently mix till bread is evenly coated. Transfer the bread pudding mixture into your greased slow cooker.
4. Cover, then cook within 3 hours on low till it's set. Cool it down, then serve.

Nutritional Values:

- Calories: 421
- Net Carbs: 54g
- Fat: 20g
- Protein: 9g
- Sugar: 16g

Difficulty: 1 2 **3** 4 5

Chocolate Chip Cookie Bars

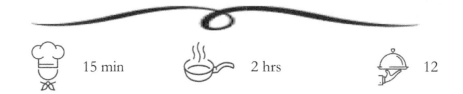

🧑‍🍳 15 min   🍳 2 hrs   🍽 12

Ingredients:

- 300g plain flour
- 5g baking soda
- 1.5g salt
- 170g unsalted butter, melted and cooled
- 200g light brown sugar
- 100g granulated sugar

- Two big eggs
- 10ml vanilla extract
- 200g chocolate chips
- Optional: 100g chopped nuts (walnuts, pecans, or almonds)

Directions:

1. Oil your slow cooker using butter.
2. In your big container, mix plain flour, baking soda, and salt. Put aside.
3. In your separate medium container, whisk butter, light brown sugar, and granulated sugar till smooth.
4. Add the eggs one at a time, whisking after each addition. Mix in vanilla extract. Combine it with the dry mixture till blended.
5. Fold in the chocolate chips and optional chopped nuts. Pour the cookie dough into your greased slow cooker insert and spread it out evenly.
6. Place a clean tea towel under your slow cooker lid to prevent condensation from dripping onto the cookie bars as they cook. Cover with the lid.
7. Cook on low within 2 hours till it's set. Cool it down, slice, then serve.

Nutritional Values:

- Calories: 388
- Net Carbs: 49g
- Fat: 19g
- Protein: 5g
- Sugar: 25g

Difficulty: 1   2   3   **4**   5

Gingerbread Pudding Cake

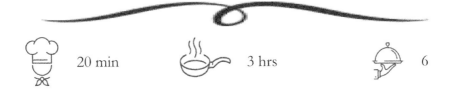

🧑‍🍳 20 min   🍳 3 hrs   🛎️ 6

Ingredients:

- 225g self-raising flour
- 2g ground ginger
- 1g ground cinnamon
- 0.5g ground nutmeg
- 50g butter, unsalted, softened
- 100g dark brown sugar
- One big egg, beaten

- 60ml golden syrup
- 60ml black treacle
- 180ml milk
- 1g bicarbonate of soda
- 250ml boiling water

Directions:

1. Grease your big slow cooker using butter or non-stick cooking spray.
2. In your medium container, whisk self-raising flour, ground ginger, cinnamon, and nutmeg.
3. In your big container, cream the softened butter with the dark brown sugar till fluffy. Add the beaten egg, then mix well.
4. Add golden syrup and black treacle to the wet ingredients while stirring.
5. Slowly add the dry ingredients to the wet mixture while stirring gently. Add in milk and continue to mix till fully combined.
6. In your small container, dissolve bicarbonate of soda in boiling water and stir into the cake batter till fully incorporated.
7. Pour the batter into your slow cooker and cover it with a lid or tea towel to prevent steam from dripping onto the cake. Cook on low within approximately 3 hours till cooked through.
8. When done cooking, carefully remove the cake, then cool it down. Serve.

Nutritional Values:

- Calories: 410
- Net Carbs: 72g
- Fat: 12g
- Protein: 6g
- Sugar: 21g

Difficulty: 1 2 3 **4** 5

Nutella Swirl Brownies

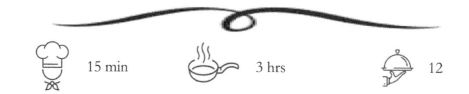

🧑‍🍳 15 min   🍳 3 hrs   🍽 12

Ingredients:

- 200g unsalted butter
- 200g dark chocolate, chopped
- 300g granulated sugar
- Three big eggs
- 5ml vanilla extract

- 200g plain flour
- 50g cocoa powder
- 1.5g salt
- 150g Nutella

Directions:

1. In your heatproof container, dissolve butter and chopped dark chocolate in the microwave. Put aside.
2. In your big container, whisk sugar, eggs, and vanilla extract till fluffy.
3. Gradually add cooled chocolate mixture to your egg mixture, then mix well.
4. Sift in the plain flour, cocoa powder, and salt. Fold gently till just combined.
5. Line your slow cooker with baking parchment or silicone liner, ensuring it covers the base and sides.
6. Pour the brownie batter into your slow cooker, then spread it out evenly.
7. Spoon dollops of Nutella on top of the brownie batter and using a knife or skewer, create swirling patterns throughout.
8. Cover, then cook within 3 hours on low till cooked through.
9. Turn off your slow cooker and let the brownies cool inside within an hour before removing them from the pot. Slice into 12 equal pieces. Serve.

Nutritional Values:

- Calories: 475
- Net Carbs: 55g
- Fat: 26g
- Protein: 6g
- Sugar: 25g

Difficulty: 1 2 3 **4** 5

Conversion Tables

Liquids*

METRIC	CUP	IMPERIAL
15ml		1.2 fl oz
30ml		1 fl oz
60ml	1/4 cup	2 fl oz
80ml	1/3 cup	2 3/4 fl oz
100ml		3 1/2 fl oz
125ml	1/2 cup	4 fl oz
150ml		5 fl oz
180ml	3/4 cup	6 fl oz
200ml		7 fl oz
250ml	1 cup	8 3/4 fl oz
310ml	1 1/4 cups	10 1/2 fl oz
375ml	1 1/2 cups	13 fl oz
430ml	1 3/4 cups	15 fl oz
475ml		16 fl oz
500ml	2 cups	17 fl oz
625ml	2 1/2 cups	21 1/2 fl oz
750ml	3 cups	26 fl oz
1L	4 cups	35 fl oz
1.25L	5 cups	44 fl oz
1.5L	6 cups	52 fl oz
2L	8 cups	70 fl oz
2.5L	10 cups	88 fl oz

Mass (weight) *

METRIC	IMPERIAL
10g	1/4oz
15g	1/2oz
30g	1oz
60g	2oz
90g	3oz
125g	4oz (1/4 lb)
155g	5oz
185g	6oz
220g	7oz
250g	8oz (1/2 lb)
280g	9oz
315g	10oz
345g	11oz
375g	12oz (3/4 lb)
410g	13oz
440g	14oz
470g	15oz
500g (1/2 kg)	16oz (1 lb)
750g	24oz (1 1/2 lb)
1kg	32oz (2 lb)
1.5kg	48oz (3 lb)
2kg	64oz (4 lb)

Oven temperatures

CELSIUS (electric)	CELSIUS (fan-forced)	FAHRENHEIT	GAS	
120°	100°	250°	1	very slow
150°	130°	300°	2	slow
160°	140°	325°	3	moderately slow
180°	160°	350°	4	moderate
190°	170°	375°	5	moderately hot
200°	180°	400°	6	hot
230°	210°	450°	7	very hot
250°	230°	500°	9	very hot

If using a fan-forced oven, your cooking time may be a little quicker, so start checking your food a little earlier.

Metric Cup and Spoon sizes*

CUP	METRIC
1/4	60ml
1/3	80ml
1/2	125ml
1 cup	250ml
SPOON	METRIC
1/4 tsp	1.25ml
1/2 tsp	2.5ml
1 tsp	5ml
1 tbsp (4 tsp)	20ml

CREDITS: *https://kitchentotable.com.au/*

Printed in Great Britain
by Amazon